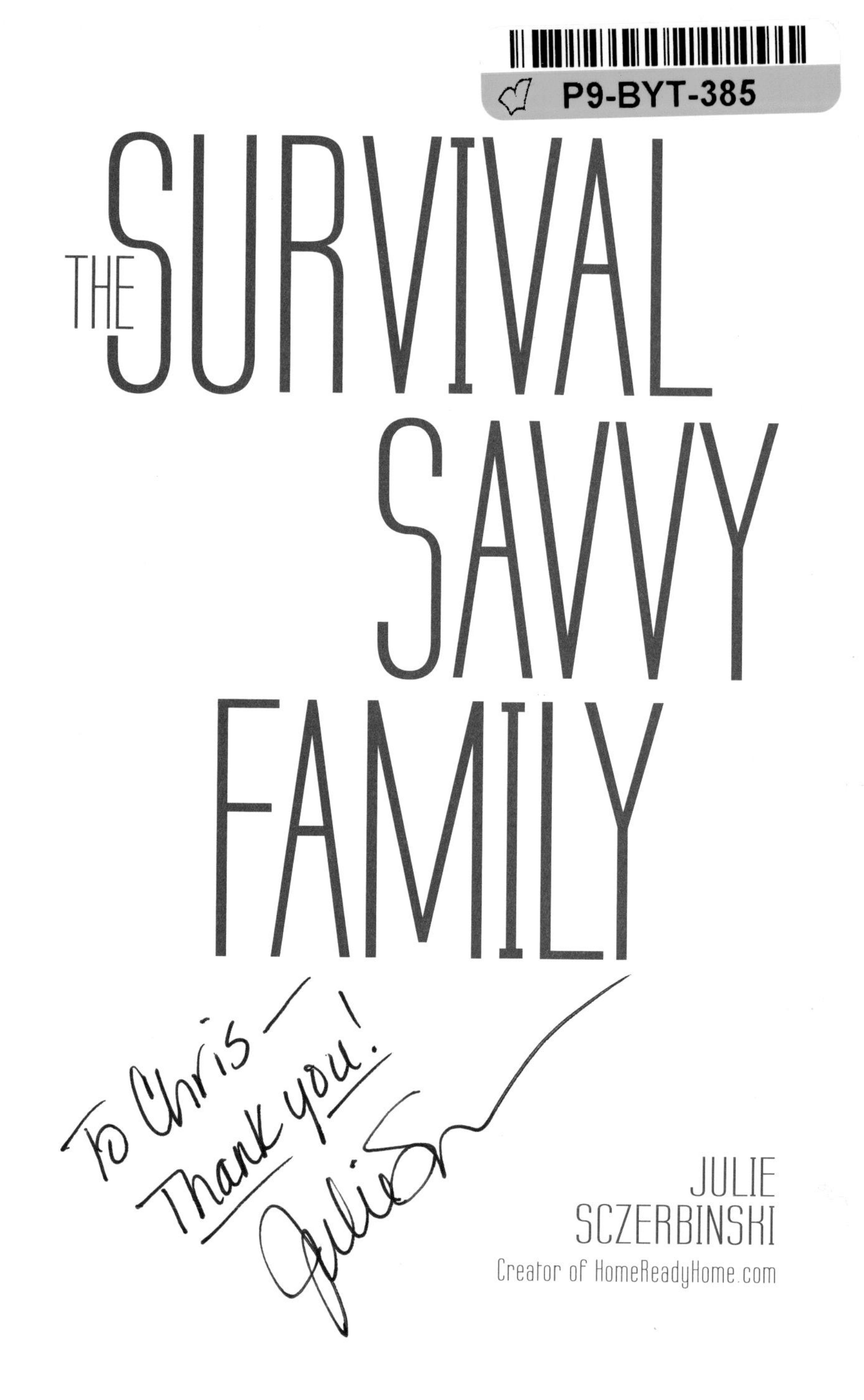
P9-BYT-385
THE SURVIVAL SAVVY FAMILY
To Chris — Thank you!
JULIE SCZERBINSKI
Creator of HomeReadyHome.com

Published by

LIVING READY fw

Living Ready, an imprint of F+W, A Content + eCommerce Company
700 East State Street • Iola, WI 54990-0001
715-445-2214 • 888-457-2873
www.livingreadyonline.com

Other fine Living Ready books are available
from your local bookstore and online suppliers.
Visit our website at www.livingreadyonline.com

ISBN-13: 9781440300042
ISBN-10: 1440300046

Cover Design by Sharon Bartsch
Designed by Jana Tappa
Edited by Paul Kennedy

Printed in USA

DEDICATION

To Pete, Sophie, and Mia

ACKNOWLEDGEMENTS

A special thank you to my husband and daughters. I appreciate the sacrifices you made so I could write this book. I love you more than words can express.

To my book writing cheerleading team: Jodi Helmer, Leanne Farrell, Bonnie Shelton, Jennifer Osuch, Jane Baldwin, Lesslie B., Bob Wray, and my parents. I'm sincerely grateful for your support and for believing in me even when I didn't. And thank you Andre at nextlevelreadiness.com for inspiring the family emergency plan template design.

A big shout out to my editor, Paul Kennedy. Thank you for your time, expert guidance and especially for the laughter. This book wouldn't be as good without you.

Thanks to Jackie Musser, Patty Dunning, and all the folks at F+W who had a hand in this project and to Angela Paskett, without you, the project may never have happened.

Lastly, a heartfelt thank you to the readers at HomeReadyHome.com for continuing to stop by with advice, tips, and humor.

CONTENTS

Introduction

If my family had to evacuate,
where would we go?

How would we have managed if our
tap water was contaminated?

What would I have **fed the kids** if we were stuck on the Atlanta interstate for ten hours like thousands were **during a winter storm?**

What exactly goes in an **emergency kit?**

I know I am not alone in my concerns. One or two of these questions have crossed your mind. Have you also had moments when you wondered what you should do if a disaster strikes while your kids are at school or worried about the possibility of a stranger luring your child into his car?

Good news. Asking these kinds of questions will bring you closer to being survival savvy. In other words, ready for whatever emergency comes your way.

Survival savvy is having a plan. It's thinking about the tough situations that no one likes to think about and then coming up with a strategy for tackling them. There are huge benefits to having a plan and living ready. Knowing what to do and how to do it reduces the danger your family faces in a disaster. Not to mention the fear and anxiety. If you have a plan, things become easier in a challenging situation.

I'd like to be able to say I've always been ready but that isn't the case. Growing up, I lived a pretty carefree life. Any plans I made revolved around school, work and friends. After college, the only thing I was ready for was marriage and a family.

Not long after my husband and I married, 9/11 happened. Like millions of Americans, I was shaken to the core. It was the first time I actually thought "what if". Then, our town officials handed out potassium iodine pills, a.k.a. nuke pills. Convinced the authorities knew something they weren't telling me, I did the only thing I could think of to prepare my family for the worst-case scenario. I threw together an emergency kit.

When the worst never happened, I put off updating the emergency kit. I had plenty of excuses why I never got around to it. My philosophy? It won't happen to us. Besides, I like to think positive. And as a mom with two kids I was far too busy to focus on another thing.

I didn't give readiness any more thought for a few years. The tipping point came when I read Chris Martenson's book, *The Crash Course*. In it, Martenson examines the sustainability of our economy, energy and environment and sums up his findings in this sentence: "Massive change is upon us."

Thinking about a changing world brought back the "what ifs". And this time my questions didn't seem so far-fetched. After all, look at hurricanes Katrina and Sandy, the tsunamis in Thailand and Japan, the earthquake in Haiti, and the

tornado in Joplin, Missouri. Those were just some of the big, newsworthy events. At the same time, I was hearing of many challenging personal situations—friends who had lost their jobs, homes and spouses. Amid all this uncertainty, the only thing I could be certain of was planning for an emergency is a wise idea.

I no longer think it won't happen to my family. Yes, most of the disasters are low probability events. But all of them are high impact events. Are you willing to gamble with your loved ones' well-being? I'm not.Taking the steps to plan and be ready is the responsible thing to do. As parents, we have little lives depending on us to care for and keep them safe. You don't want to be caught in a crisis with your children, thinking *if only I had planned for this.*

I'm still a positive thinker. Being ready doesn't change that. Making a plan for negative events doesn't mean you are attracting them into your life. Buying car insurance and wearing your seat belt doesn't guarantee you a car accident, does it?

And I've discovered planning for a disaster doesn't take as much time as I

I'd like to be able to say I've always been ready but that isn't the case. Growing up, I lived a pretty carefree life. Any plans I made revolved around school, work, and friends. After college, the only thing I was ready for was marriage and a family.

originally thought. Once your plans are in place, the time commitment is minimal. A few minutes, a few times a year to review plans, practice and rotate supplies. In between, it's business as usual. It really is easy, but you have to be vigilant. Pay attention to what's going on around you and what's happening in the news.

I know it all can seem overwhelming at first. Fear not. I'm here to help you start. The first two chapters will show you how to make a family emergency plan and what to include in an emergency kit. Next, you'll find tips on food and water storage, first aid, and financial planning. We'll go over how to be ready when you are on the go, at the office or on vacation. Then I'll cover how to plan for power outages, natural disasters, house fires, and home invasions. Throughout we'll discuss ways to help your kids be ready, including how to be sure they stay safe at school, in the neighborhood, and online. By the end of the book you will be well on your way to becoming survival savvy.

Sound good? Now turn the page and let's get started.

CHAPTER 1

Family Emergency Plan

Is your family's emergency plan a disaster? If so, you're not alone. Sixty percent of Americans say being ready for emergencies is very important, but less than 20% of us really are ready. Unfortunately, knowing you should be ready won't offer your family the same protection as actually taking the steps to be ready. What's the first step? **Make a plan before disaster strikes.**

Let's imagine for a moment the kids are at school and your spouse is at work. You're just about to run to the store to pick up a few things for dinner when you hear a knock at the front door. A policeman stands on your front step and he says there's been an accident not too far from your neighborhood. A train carrying crude oil derailed and exploded. Hazardous smoke is heading your way and you must leave immediately. Imagine how panicked you'd feel because you have no idea what to do! Having an emergency plan will help you stay calm under pressure and take the necessary action to keep you and your family safe.

What Should You Plan For?

Before you can create a plan you have to figure out what you need to plan for. Start by making a list of all the potential emergencies that could affect your family. Think about personal disasters, such as losing your job. Then think about disasters that would impact your neighborhood or town, like a chemical spill or a hurricane. If you're struggling to identify the possibilities, ask your local emergency management office to give you some ideas of the risks for your area. You may feel a little paranoid planning for every disaster imaginable, but wouldn't you rather have a plan for something that never happens than be caught off guard without one?

Making Your Plan

Schedule a family meeting to gather everyone together. With my family's busy schedule, finding 20 minutes where we were together in the same room seemed almost impossible. If you have the same challenge, schedule several mini-meetings. It can be a formal have-a-seat-at-the-dining- room-table gathering or an informal let's-go-grab-some-ice-cream meeting. Either way, try to make it fun. A plan is just another family conversation. It doesn't have to be complicated or boring.

Once everyone's together, talk about each of the disasters you've identified as possible risks. Discuss the different ways your family would be notified of the emergency—alarms, radio or television alerts, text alerts or sirens—and make sure everyone knows what each warning system sounds like. Also, does everyone know what to do when they hear the warning?

Outline the action steps your family would need to take before, during and after each situation. Chapter 9 gives you the before, during and after steps for some of the more likely natural disasters. You can also find information at Ready.gov and the American Red Cross. Remember, disasters never sleep, so make sure you talk about how your plan might change depending on the time of day or night.

After you've determined the action steps, give each family member a job to do. Who will call for help? Who will grab the emergency supplies? Who will put Fluffy in her cat carrier? Teamwork is essential in an emergency.

Make a Plan for When Your Family's Apart

If your family is anything like mine, there aren't too many hours in the day when everyone is together in one place, so assume your family will be separated when disaster strikes. Ask your workplace and your children's schools about emergency procedures and request copies of any plans.

Think of all the places you frequent and then come up with additional action plans. What will you do if you're in line at Starbucks and you receive a tornado warning alert on your cell phone? What should your children do if there's a fire at school? How will you get home from work if you're caught in a freak ice storm during rush hour?

HOW TO KEEP IN TOUCH

There's no question being separated from your loved ones in a crisis will cause you to feel anxious. In normal times, our first thought is "I'll just call them on the phone."

WHICH DISASTER SHOULD YOU PLAN FOR?

PERSONAL DISASTERS

- Job loss
- House fire
- Serious illness
- Death of a family member

NATURAL DISASTERS

- Winter storms
- Severe thunderstorms
- Droughts
- Hurricanes
- Tornadoes
- Floods
- Wildfires
- Landslides
- Earthquakes
- Tsunamis
- Volcanoes
- Epidemics

MAN-MADE DISASTERS

- Chemical spills
- Blackouts
- Nuclear accidents
- Terrorism

In a disaster, land lines and local cell phone towers may be damaged or overwhelmed by the volume of calls and your call won't go through. What will you do?

Many times, you'll still be able to make long distance calls. Choose two out-of-area friends or relatives you could contact to let them know where you are and that you're OK. In past disasters, people were also able to send text messages to stay in touch, so choose someone who is well versed in technology and knows how to text. Likewise, if you have a member of the family who is texting-challenged, include a texting tutorial as part of your family plan meeting.

WHERE TO MEET

Now that you know how you'll contact one another, you need to choose a safe place to meet in case going home isn't an option. Pick a location outside of your neighborhood that everyone knows how to get to—one of your kids' schools, your church, the police department, even a grocery store. You'll also want to decide on a meeting place right outside your home in case of emergency like a house fire.

Divorced Family Plans

Do both parents have complete medical histories on all the children as well as copies of their health insurance cards? If one of the kids is injured, will both

WATCH VS. WARNING

The National Weather Service alerts use the terms watch and warning. Knowing the difference between these two words can save your life.

- **WATCH means keep your eyes open and stay aware.** Weather conditions are right for a severe weather event—tornado, hurricane, flood—to occur near you at any moment.
- **WARNING means danger is approaching!** A specific weather threat is happening right now and is heading your way.

parents notify each other on the way to the doctor or will the call come after treatment has already been given?

Who will pick up the kids from school if there is an unexpected emergency? Will it always be the same parent or will it depend on whom the child is staying with at the time of the event?

What if one or both parent's homes are destroyed in a major disaster?

These are a few of the details divorced families need to work out in advance. Additionally, both parents need to be kept up-to-date with changes in emergency contact information, such as a new work or cell phone number.

It may not be easy to talk with your ex, but it's essential you have a discussion about your emergency plans. Set aside your differences and keep one goal in mind—the safety and well-being of your kids.

Plans for Family Members with Special Needs

Family emergency plans that include elderly family members or those with special needs require some extra thought and planning. Start by writing down everything you or your family member need on a day-to-day basis during normal times. Then think about how these needs could be impacted during different emergency situations.

Are there items like medications, medical devices, spare batteries or eyeglasses that you'll need to stock up on? Talk to your doctor and ask about getting an extra supply.

Does your family member receive special services like meals delivered to them at home or dialysis on a regular basis? If so, ask the organizations providing the special service about their emergency plans and consider how it applies to you or your relative.

How will the family member's special needs affect your ability to evacuate in an emergency? Determine in advance where you will go and how you will get there.

Does your relative have a medical alert bracelet to help first responders identify his special medical needs? How about a medical alert system that allows him to call for help? If not, consider getting one.

Who is available to help you during an emergency? Remember, a disaster could strike without warning. What would you do if you're across town and you're prevented from getting to the person you care for? Put together a support team. Is there a trusted neighbor or friend you could call on for assistance? Ask your local emergency officials about a special needs registry. Some communities have programs that offer emergency assistance to residents who are pre-registered.

It's also a good idea to compile all vital medical information for the person with special needs into a folder that you'll keep with your plan. You'll want to include a medical history, a list of all medications and dosage information, a description of medical devices including model numbers, contact information for all doctors and caregivers, and copies of insurance or Medicare cards. Once you have gathered all the information, deliver a copy to your trusted support team along with a spare house key.

Pet Plans

Your pet is part of your family, and as such is relying on you in an emergency.

A good place to start is to make sure your pets have identification in case you become separated. Do all your pets wear collars with ID tags? Schedule an appointment with your vet to have a microchip implanted in them. As tiny as a grain of rice, a microchip is an identification device your veterinarian implants under your pet's skin usually between the shoulder blades. It's a simple, painless procedure similar to receiving a vaccine. If your pet is lost, an animal shelter or vet hospital employee can use a hand-held wand to scan and retrieve your contact information. That's why it's so important that you keep the emergency contact information tied to your pet's microchip up-to-date.

Determine a safe pet-friendly place to stay in the event you have to evacuate. Do you have an out-of-area friend or relative who is willing to house your family, including your pet? Make a list of the names and phone numbers of pet-loving friends, pet-friendly hotels, veterinary hospitals and boarding kennels outside of your local area and keep this information with your emergency plan. Check out www.petswelcome.com if you need help finding pet friendly hotels and more. Also, check with your local authorities to find out what kind of shelter options, if any, will be provided in an emergency.

Lastly, if a disaster strikes when you're not at home, is there someone who would be willing to go to your house, pick up your pets and care for them until you return? Make arrangements with this trusted neighbor or friend and make sure they have a spare key or another way to gain access to your home.

Put Your Plan On Paper

The easiest way for everyone to remember all this information is to write it down, creating one master emergency plan.

Grab a piece of paper or use the templates in this book and write down your out-of-area contacts' names and phone numbers as well as your agreed upon meeting places. It's a good idea to copy that same information down onto a wallet size card for each family member to have with them at all times.

You'll also want to include contact information for all family members as well as trusted friends or neighbors on your master plan. Then, jot down the direct phone number to the police and fire departments as well as ambulance, doctors and hospitals because you may have difficulty getting through to 911 in a large-scale disaster.

Because your master plan is designed to be an "all-hazards" plan, you'll want to include details on your cars, utilities, insurance policies—any pertinent information you could possibly need at your fingertips.

Once you've written it all down, decide on a safe place to store your plan. I highly recommend you make a copy to keep with your emergency supplies and post the important phone numbers on your refrigerator or inside of a kitchen cabinet door.

Lastly, set a date to review your plan. Yearly reviews are a smart idea and if any major change happens before the next date—a new job or a new family member—make sure to update your plan.

Practice Makes Perfect

Now that we've had a discussion and wrote down the important information, we're done right? Not quite.

As parents, we're well aware of how important it is to practice. At times, it may seem like your life revolves around practice, from carting one child to soccer practice to reminding the other to practice for the upcoming piano recital to helping both with homework assignments at night. We know if we are going to completely understand and remember something, we have to practice.

Practicing your emergency plan as little as two times a year will keep everyone in your family familiar with the procedures you put in place. It will help you see if your plan works by identifying holes you couldn't have predicted in the planning stages. Most importantly, practicing the plan will give you the chance to see if everyone understands what he or she is supposed to do or if additional training is necessary. Practice will reduce the time you spend thinking in an emergency situation, which in turn gives you more time to act when every second counts.

When you change your clocks in the spring and fall, review your plan's procedures and run mock drills for fire, earthquakes, hurricanes—all the dangers you identified. Start the stopwatch and time how long it takes you to get through each scenario safely without sacrificing accuracy. Practice gathering and carrying your emergency supplies. Run your drills morning, noon and night with the lights on and lights off. Schedule a no-power weekend. Talk about the conditions your family will experience that you can't simulate in drills, such as smoke or falling furniture, so everyone will have an idea of what to expect in a real disaster.

Afterwards, get together and review. Discuss what worked and what didn't, then make adjustments to your plan. The time you spend now practicing will save you time spent thinking in an emergency situation and give you more time to act when every second counts.

How to Shut off Your Utilities

Know where the main shut off valves are for all the utilities and knowing how to turn them off is common-sense advice, yet many of us don't pay attention to it. We think *if it ever needs to be done, I'll deal with it then.*

It wasn't until a contractor needed to shut the water off to work on the plumbing in our first house that my family realized we needed to take this advice more seriously. After a 30-minute search for the main water shut-off valve—we looked in the garage, emptied closets, and asked neighbors where their valves were located, hoping ours would be in the same place—we found it behind some garage shelving. We overlooked it the first time because it was painted the same color as the wall. Imagine the destruction if water had been pouring out of a ruptured pipe flooding the house that whole time!

It's essential you know when to power down the utilities and how to do it *quickly.* Immediately after a disaster, electrical sparks can ignite leaking gas, causing an explosion, cracked water lines can result in polluted water flowing through your tap and yes, water from ruptured pipes can flood your home.

Don't wait until you're faced with a disaster, locate the main shut off valves now for all utilities, mark them and if needed, post detailed how-to instructions nearby. Then make sure all responsible family members know where they are and how to turn them off.

HOW TO TURN OFF THE ELECTRICITY

Locate the main circuit panel in your home. It's usually found on an interior wall near the electrical meter. Sometimes there will be a main switch by the meter on the outside of your home, so make sure you have located all panels.

In the event of an emergency, switch all the individual breakers to the off position first, then the main breaker. Remember: Never step in standing water to access the fuse box without calling an electrician for advice first.

HOW TO TURN OFF THE WATER

Find the main water shut-off valve inside your home. Test it to make sure it can be completely turned off as sometimes the valves are rusted and will break when you try to turn them. Once you're sure it works, label it for easy identification.

There should also be an outside shut-off valve curbside in a meter box set in the ground. The easiest way to turn the valve is with a special tool called a curb key, which is available at home improvement stores.

BE READY! YES, THERE'S AN APP FOR THAT.

POCKET FIRST AID & CPR

This American Heart Association app helped save a life in Haiti. After the earthquake, Dan Woolley survived 65 hours trapped in rubble using the Pocket First Aid & CPR's step-by-step instructions to guide him as he applied first aid to his wounds. The Respond Now! feature takes you directly to an emergency response sequence, including how-to videos, for whatever medical emergency you're facing.

Compatibility: Android and iPhone

AMERICAN RED CROSS'

TORNADO, HURRICANE, FLOOD, WILDFIRES OR EARTHQUAKE

This family of apps by the American Red Cross helps you to be ready with step-by-step instructions on what to do before, during and after different types of disasters. Download all the apps or only the one specific to the disaster your family will most likely encounter. You'll receive alerts to storms heading your way as well as have access to up-to-the-minute info on nearby shelters. The app even has emergency tools—a flashlight, alarm, strobe light and an "I'm Safe" feature that sends a message via Facebook, Twitter, text or email letting friends and family know you're okay.

Compatibility: Android and iPhone

HOW TO TURN OFF THE GAS

Look for the main shut-off valve near where the gas line enters the house. In most cases, it will be by the gas meter and components. To turn the valve ninety degrees to the off position, you'll need a wrench or large pliers. You may want to store the correct tool, pre-adjusted, right next to the valve.

Turn off the valve only if you smell gas or hear a blowing or hissing sound. Once it's been turned off, never turn it back on. It requires a qualified professional for the job, so always call your gas company for assistance.

AMERICAN RED CROSS SHELTER VIEW

Available for iPhones only, this app maps the locations of open shelters across the United States. Click on the location to read up-to-date details on each shelter, such as address and location, the specific disaster the shelter is associated with, shelter capacity and how many people are there currently looking for assistance.

Compatibility: iPhone only

FEMA

The Federal Emergency Management Agency app offers disaster safety tips, a handy list function for creating an emergency kit, and a place to store your designated emergency contacts. Also, you're able to get information and directions to your state's FEMA shelters and disaster recovery centers should the need arise.

Compatibility: Android and iPhone

PET FIRST AID

This app by American Red Cross will help you take care of Fluffy and Fido with veterinary advice for administering medication and addressing behavior problems. There are step-by-step first aid instructions, including videos, for more than two-dozen pet emergency situations. Store your vet's contact information and use the app to locate the nearest emergency vet hospital and pet-friendly hotels.

Compatibility: Android and iPhone

NOAA WEATHER RADIO HD

In addition to detailed weather forecasts and radar for your chosen location, this app sends you around the clock notifications of the latest weather warnings, watches and alerts from the National Oceanic and Atmospheric Administration even when your phone is asleep.

Compatibility: Android and iPhone

GET YOUR **KIDS INVOLVED** IN THE PLAN!

Big or small, your kids should have a part in the emergency plan! Here are seven ways to include them:

1. **HELP YOUR LITTLE ONES MEMORIZE THE FAMILY FACTS.** If you and your child become separated, authorities will have an easier time reuniting you if your child knows his full name, your full name, your home address and phone number. Be creative. Make a song out of the information or play rhyming games to help him remember.

2. **TEACH YOUR CHILD HOW AND WHEN TO DIAL 911.** And teach them when **not** to call. Make sure your little ones know what a true emergency is. Talk about the kinds of questions 911 operators ask and make sure they understand this is one stranger they can talk to and share personal information with.

3. **GET YOUR KIDS' INPUT.** Kids who help create a plan are more likely to remember it. Ask your child for ideas on family meeting places and what kind of items the family needs in an emergency. Get them involved in the discussion during the planning process and let them offer opinions on how effective they think the plan will be.

4. **GIVE YOUR CHILD A JOB TO DO.** Assign your child an age-appropriate responsibility to keep her from feeling helpless in an emergency. Even the littlest ones can manage a simple task, like turning on the television or radio for emergency updates.

5. **INTRODUCE YOUR KIDS TO YOUR EMERGENCY CONTACTS.** If your child doesn't already know your emergency contacts personally, set up a time when they can meet. Also, it's a good idea to occasionally remind young children of the connection. If you happen to see or talk to the contact, you might say something like, "Do you remember Mom's friend, Amy Smith? She's your friend, too and will help us if there's an emergency."

6. **PLAY MAKE-BELIEVE.** One of the easiest ways to help kids remember what to do in an emergency is to pretend the emergency is happening. Before you practice, be sure your children are aware it's not a real emergency, then always make the drills fun. For example, let your kids take turns being in charge of conducting the drills or set off the fire alarm and give a prize to the first child to reach the family meeting spot.

7. **QUIZ YOUR KIDS.** The car is a great place to have conversations with your children. Use the driving time together to ask younger children basic questions. Where do we go when we hear the fire alarm? What number do we call when we need help? As your children get older, ask more complicated questions about their response to different scenarios. You might ask something like, "What would you do if you arrived home from school and found me passed out on the floor?" Or, "What would you do if you're at your friend's house and you hear a tornado warning alert on the radio?"

DISCUSSION QUESTIONS: GET YOUR FAMILY TALKING ABOUT YOUR EMERGENCY PLAN

- What type of disaster is most likely to happen in our area?
- Does everyone know how to prepare for the disaster?
- Does everyone know what to do if the disaster occurs?
- What resources or agencies can give us more information about how to plan an appropriate response to the disaster?
- Does everyone know the safe spots inside or outside of our home for each type of disaster that could occur?
- What kind of emergency alert system does our community have?
- What does the emergency alert sound like?
- What should we do when we hear the emergency alert?
- What radio or TV stations broadcast emergency info for our area?
- If there are members of the family with special needs, are they able to receive emergency alerts or do they need a special tool to assist them?
- Are there agencies available to assist the family members with special needs during an emergency?
- Have we registered for their assistance program?
- Where are the evacuation routes in our community?
- Have we mapped the routes on Mapquest, Google Maps or GPS?
- If evacuation is necessary, does each family member know what task they are responsible for and understand what's expected of them?
- Where would we evacuate to?
- If the roads aren't passable, what's our secondary evacuation plan?
- What is the school's emergency plan or disaster procedure?
- For working family members, what's the emergency plan or disaster procedure at the workplace?

- Are all emergency telephone numbers posted by the phone?
- Does everyone in the family know when and how to call 911?
- Do all cell phone users have an "In Case of Emergency" contact filed under the word ICE in their contacts list, so first responders would know who to call?
- Do all adults have a Living Will and/or Healthcare Power of Attorney?
- Do we have adequate insurance—life, auto, home, flood?
- In case we're separated during a sudden emergency, like a house fire, where is the family meeting place right outside of the house?
- Where is the family meeting place outside of the neighborhood, in case we can't return home?
- Who are the out-of-area contact persons for our family?
- Does everyone know how to contact them?
- Does everyone know where the main switches to all the utilities are located?
- Does everyone know when and how to turn the utilities off?
- Does each family member know what the smoke detector, carbon monoxide and burglar alarms sounds like?
- Does everyone know what to do if the smoke detector, carbon monoxide and burglar alarms go off?
- Have we planned at least two escape routes from each room of the house?
- Is at least one person in the family certified in first aid and CPR?
- Do we have all family records stored in a water and fireproof container?
- Do our pets have tags and microchips for identification purposes?
- If we have to evacuate, which family member will be responsible for gathering our pets?
- Is our evacuation spot a pet-friendly place?
- If not, what will we do with our pets?
- If we can't make it home, who will be available to care for or evacuate our pets?
- When will we get together again to review and/or make changes to this plan?

FAMILY EMERGENCY PLAN

Using a pencil, complete all sections below. Review the information annually and update if necessary.

Family Last Name: ______________________________

Household Address: ______________________________

____

Home Phone: ______________________________

FAMILY/HOUSEHOLD MEMBERS INFORMATION

NAME	RELATION	BIRTHDATE	SOCIAL SECURITY NO.

PET INFORMATION

NAME	TYPE/COLOR	LICENSE NO.	RABIES VACCINATION NO.

HOUSEHOLD INFORMATION

	MAKE	MODEL	YEAR	LICENSE PLATE NO.	VIN NO.
VEHICLE #1					
VEHICLE #2					
VEHICLE #3					

	UTILITY COMPANY	PHONE	ACCOUNT NO.
GAS			
ELECTRIC			
WATER			
PHONE			
CABLE			
OTHER			

	INSURANCE COMPANY	PHONE	POLICY NO.
AUTO			
HOME/RENTERS			
MEDICAL			
LIFE			
OTHER			

EMERGENCY CONTACT NUMBERS

EMERGENCY NUMBERS

In Case of an Emergency: CALL 911

If 911 is not working, call the following numbers:

Police: ______________________________

Fire: ______________________________

Ambulance: ______________________________

Hospital: ______________________________

Poison Control: 1-800-222-1222 (US residents) ______________________________

OTHER IMPORTANT NUMBERS

	NAME	PHONE
DOCTOR		
DOCTOR		
DOCTOR		
DENTIST		
PHARMACY		
VETERINARIAN		

FAMILY CONTACT INFORMATION

NAME	CELL PHONE	WORK PHONE	EMAIL

FRIENDS AND NEIGHBORS CONTACT INFORMATION

NAME	ADDRESS	PHONE	EMAIL

OUT-OF-AREA CONTACTS

If our family is separated and unable to contact each other after a disaster, call the predetermined out-of-area contacts and report your location and condition.

Out-of-Area Contact #1

Name: ______________________

Address: ______________________

Home Phone: ______________________

Work Phone: ______________________

Cell Phone: ______________________

Email: ______________________

Out-of-Area Contact #2

Name: ______________________

Address: ______________________

Home Phone: ______________________

Work Phone: ______________________

Cell Phone: ______________________

Email: ______________________

EMERGENCY PLAN PROCEDURES

If our family is separated after a disaster, meet at the following predetermined locations:

Outside of Home Location:____

____

Outside of Neighborhood Location: ____________________________________

Address: ____

Phone: ____

Directions: ____

____

____

____

____

WORKPLACE AND SCHOOL EMERGENCY PLANS

Complete the section below and attach copies of employer and school emergency plans.

1. Family Member's Name: ______________________

❑ Work ❑ School ❑ Other: ______________________

Address: ______________________

____

Phone: ______________________

Meeting Location: ______________________

____

Procedures: ______________________

____

____

2. Family Member's Name: ______________________

❑ Work ❑ School ❑ Other: ______________________

Address: ______________________

____

Phone: ______________________

Meeting Location: ______________________

____

Procedures: ______________________

____

____

3. Family Member's Name: ______________________

❑ Work ❑ School ❑ Other: ______________________

Address: ______________________

____

Phone: ______________________

Meeting Location: ______________________

____

Procedures: ______________________

____

____

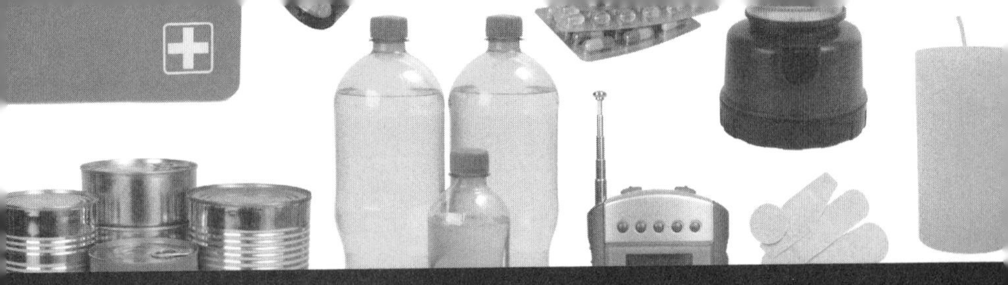

CHAPTER 2

The Emergency Kit

For more than three decades, it has been drilled into us—

If there's an emergency, call 911. So, it's hard to imagine dialing 911 and not getting response. But the truth is, in a disaster, help may not be available right away. Local first responders could be stretched to the limit trying to deal with the number of requests for assistance, plus it takes time for relief organizations to mobilize and come to your aid. This is the reason emergency management officials offer this advice: **Be prepared to take care of yourself for a minimum of three days.** A pre-packed emergency kit ready to use when things go haywire will help you to do just that.

Build an Emergency Kit

An emergency kit contains the essential supplies your family needs to survive for 72 hours and it must be portable. Some disasters, like hurricanes, come with advanced warning but others, such as chemical spills or wildfires happen suddenly, forcing you to leave your home with only a moment's notice. In the chaos of the unexpected evacuation, you won't have the mindset to remember everything you need to take with you or the time to collect it. That's why a pre-packed emergency kit as opposed to an emergency closet needs to be in your home.

Before you grab that giant Rubbermaid tote and get to packing, let me suggest you build your kit with a solid foundation—in the form of a Go-Bag.

What is a Go-Bag?

A Go-Bag is a mini emergency kit for each member of your family and it's the most important part of your family emergency kit. Catch an episode of any of the survival reality TV shows and you're bound to hear someone mention the *Rules of Three*: You can live three hours without shelter. You can live three days without water. You can live three weeks without food. Go-Bags are packed with the *Rules of Three* in mind—in other words, they are stocked with the bare necessities for survival.

Because emergencies are unpredictable, your ability to improvise or adapt is crucial to your family's well-being. Don't assume in a crisis, you'll always have the luxury of evacuating with a car load of supplies. What happens if rubble from an earthquake or a traffic jam caused by a mass exodus forces you to leave your car behind and walk to a safe destination? Or what would you do if the only way to escape rising flood waters was by rescue boat? Would you be able to carry your extra large kit containing *all* the emergency supplies for your entire family? Probably not. That's why I suggest you pack *part* of your emergency kit in a Go-Bag so you'll never be left without the very basic life-supporting supplies.

Choose your Bag Wisely

Forget the videos you've seen. You know, the ones with the celebrity spokesperson piling canned food, water and a weather radio into a huge plastic tote before closing the lid. They break the first rule of packing a Go-Bag which is it *must* be easy to carry.

Resist the temptation to use that giant plastic tote or even a suitcase with wheels and go with a backpack instead. Backpacks are lightweight plus they allow you to travel hands free. And because they're on your back, they are easy to maneuver. You will never have to worry about how you'll drag your supplies over rough terrain.

How Much Stuff Can You Carry?

The general consensus among backpackers is carry no more than 25% of your body weight. For example, if you weigh 200 pounds, your backpack should weigh 50 pounds tops. While this gives you a starting point, in general, the size and weight of your Go-Bag will depend on your build, your age and any physical limitations like a bad back or bum knee.

BUY OR **DIY?**

There's no shortage of companies offering pre-made Go-Bags for sale. You may be tempted to purchase one and be done with it. Resist the urge until you do your homework. Not all of the sellers are looking out for your best interests. Plus a one-size-fits-all Go-Bag may not address your family's specific needs. In that case, it will be wiser to make your own. Ask yourself these questions before you buy a Go-Bag:

- Are the items good quality or are they made cheaply?
- Are all of the supplies listed in the description actually included in the bag?
- Does the Go-Bag have enough food and water for my family?
- Will my family eat the food?
- Can I purchase the same supplies for less money elsewhere?
- Do I know how to use the contents of the bag?
- What additional items do I need to customize it for my family?

Most importantly, don't over-pack. I'm the girl who has over-packed for every trip I've ever taken so subscribing to this idea was hard for me in the beginning, too. But remember survival is just that—survival—and it isn't meant to be comfortable. Think *life preserver*, not *convenience store*. Don't pack as if you're on your way to spend a weekend at some posh resort.

What to Pack

When you are choosing the supplies to include in your Go-Bag, you want to make sure you have your basic needs covered. Remember the *Rules of Three*? When I was assembling Go-Bags for my family, I found it helpful to group the supplies into eight categories: water, food, shelter, fire, first aid, hygiene, tools and emergency supplies. Let's take a look at what goes in each one.

WATER

Anything you read about emergency kits almost always says the same thing: you need to have at least a gallon of water per person per day. My first thought when I read this? *How the heck will I be able to carry three gallons of water plus everything else I need for three days?* Followed immediately by, *There's no way my kids could do it!*

With one gallon of water weighing just over eight pounds, it's unreasonable to think you can carry the recommended supply (25 pounds!) of water in your Go-Bag and walk for more than a very short distance. Therefore, I recommend you pack your Go-Bag with the bare minimum of water needed to survive.

→ PACK THE BARE MINIMUM

You can live for three days without water, so technically the bare minimum is none—although, I don't advise you go that route. Dehydration is dangerous. What starts as dizziness and headaches quickly ends in poor decision making, sickness and, even death.

We've all heard the *drink eight 8-oz glasses of water a day* health advice. If you're like me and you rarely meet that quota, you know you can live on less. The minimum your body needs to be hydrated enough to function is one liter per day. One liter times three days is three liters—a good starting point for your Go-Bag. And just as you don't store all your eggs in one basket, don't store all your water in one container. Pack three liters of water in three separate containers in your bag. By doing this, you will distribute the weight in your pack making it easier to carry.

You'll also have some water insurance in case one of your containers breaks or gets lost during the crisis.

Depending on the weather and how much energy you're exerting, three liters will disappear quickly. That's why you'll want to ration your water wisely and have at least two options in your bag for purifying any water you may find.

There are several ways of making questionable water drinkable. Boiling is the oldest method and a surefire way of purifying contaminated water, however it's not the most convenient. You need the right container, a fire source and time, which isn't always available in a pinch. Instead, I recommend you add water purification tablets and a water filtration system to your Go-Bag.

→ WATER PURIFICATION TABLETS

Water purification tablets, also known as water disinfection tabs, are effervescent tablets that destroy disease causing micro-organisms in water. You fill your container with contaminated water, drop the tab in and wait the full amount of time specified on the package. Depending on the brand of tablets, it could take up to four hours to work, so it's important that you follow the directions exactly.

→ WATER FILTRATION SYSTEMS

There's no shortage of water filters to choose from—hand pump filters, water bottles with built-in filters and straws with filters attached. These are all similar in idea to the Brita Pitcher Filter many of us have in sitting in our refrigerators, but they are way more powerful. These "certified purifiers" clean the water by removing 99.99% of Cryptosporidium and Giardia, two of the leading causes of waterborne gastrointestinal illness in the United States.

It's worth noting that while these filters take care of nasty bacteria and protozoa, used alone they don't offer protection against waterborne viruses. The water in the United States and Canada is usually free of viruses, but if you have any concerns about safety, use both the filter and the purification tablets on the water in question.

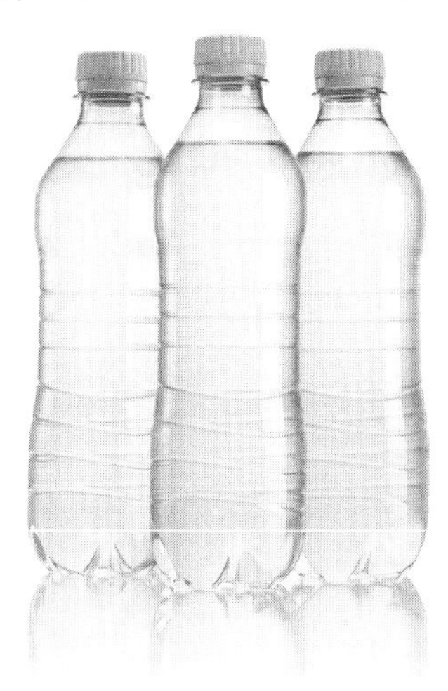

FOOD

Would it surprise you to learn food is not the top priority when you are packing your Go-Bag? Experts can't say exactly how long humans can live without food, but the general consensus is about three weeks. So, if Go-Bags are meant to hold you over for 72 hours until you can get to a safe location or help arrives, then technically, you don't need to pack any food at all. However, not eating for three days would leave you feeling pretty uncomfortable. You may feel light-headed, tired, weak, and you'll probably have a hard time concentrating. And if you're like me, missing a meal will make you down right crabby! Is that how you want to feel as you navigate through a disaster?

On the other hand, I've seen plenty of food lists for Go-Bags that seem more suited for a tailgate party than for a survival scenario. Is it realistic to think you can carry that much food on your back along with your other supplies if you were forced to evacuate on foot? Something's gotta give and food is one area where you can be a little flexible.

→ WHAT FOOD TO PACK

What should you pack in your Go-Bags? First of all, skip the commonly recommended canned fruits and vegetables. Cans are bulky and heavy—not practical in a Go-Bag because you'll be carrying it on your back.

The food you want to include is light weight, high in calories, has a long shelf life and requires little to no preparation. Look for stuff you can just tear open and eat. Protein meal bars, trail mix, peanut butter, beef jerky, tuna packets, crackers and nuts are all great Go-Bag food. In my family's bags, I packed several different varieties of protein bars for breakfast, lunch and dinner and then tossed in my kids' favorite snack items, goldfish, almonds, and peanut butter crackers.

You may be thinking *that sounds like a bunch of preservatives* and you are right. But a life or death situation is not the time to stick to your special diets unless you have a true medical condition. Hang up the Paleo and Weight Watchers and look at the big picture. Skipping three days of organic, whole foods eating won't cause as much harm as not eating, period.

SHELTER

Whether it's hot or cold outside, you will need to protect yourself from the elements. Hypothermia and hyperthermia are no joke, so it's crucial that the clothing packed in your Go-Bag is suitable to your climate. Pack a complete change of clothes including a light-weight, long-sleeve shirt, a pair of pants that could be cut into shorts (No jeans please!), two pairs of socks and two pair of underwear, and a pullover (preferably fleece) for added warmth. In winter months make sure you rotate in hats, gloves and a winter jacket.

Also, be sure to include a roll of paracord and a tarp large enough to create a make-shift shelter. I know what you're thinking. *Seriously? I'll never have to sleep outside.* I certainly hope you don't, but if there's anything we can learn from past disasters it's never say never.

FIRE

Long before Weber grills and HVAC systems, humans relied on fire to cook and to stay warm. During a disaster, fire can be used for those purposes as well as for sanitizing water, signaling for help, sterilizing first aid equipment and keeping bugs away. Therefore, no emergency kit would be complete without a way to make fire.

I'm sure you have seen at least one movie where a lone survivor is barely hanging on and all he has to start a fire is a soggy book of matches with one match inside. A supply of the more durable strike anywhere matches stored in a waterproof container, plus a lighter stored in several different pockets of your Go-Bag will prevent you from becoming that guy.

BE READY QUICK TIP!

Keep the military saying "Two is one and one is none" in mind as you gather up your emergency supplies. **Redundancy is good.** For example, each adult Go-Bag could include a pocket knife and duct tape. You could pack a hand crank cell phone charger in one and a solar cell phone charger in the other. If you pack more than one of the same item, or have multiple ways of getting the task at hand accomplished, you'll have some protection against Murphy's law, "Anything that can go wrong, will go wrong."

FIRST AID

Doesn't it seem like you can't make it through a week without one of the kids getting banged up? Don't assume things will be different in a crisis. Your Go-Bag needs to have a first aid kit, sized right for your family, as well as a good first aid manual. And if anyone in your family relies on medication, be sure you have extra prescriptions stored in your pack.

HYGIENE

A disaster isn't the time to be worried about looking your best but there are a few items you should keep in your Go-Bag to make life just a little more pleasant. Start with toilet paper. You'll also want to include a few items to keep you disease-free, such as hand sanitizer and disinfecting wipes.

TOOLS AND EMERGENCY SUPPLIES

In a large scale disaster, it's pretty much a given that the conveniences we take for granted will be severely limited or non existent. Lights, ATMs, GPS and television will have to be replaced with flashlights, cash, maps and a good book or magazine, so pack accordingly.

WATERPROOF YOUR GO-BAG

When it rains it pours and disasters have been known to be pretty wet. Nothing will seem worse than reaching into your Go-Bag for a dry set of clothes only to find out all of the pack's contents are soaked. You can waterproof your Go-Bag one of two ways. Purchase dry bags, pouches or cases from the camping section of your local sporting goods store or make your own. For DIY protection, seal your clothes and supplies inside of freezer grade Ziploc bags. Then, line the inside of your Go-Bag with a construction grade trash bag. Add the sealed items and tie the garbage bag shut.

The Extra Supplies Stash

Once your Go-Bags are packed, start thinking about other items for your extra supplies stash. This portion of your kit should be made up of items you would consider lucky to have and not deadly if you don't. Feel free to use the container of your choice to store these items. My family has a few plastic totes filled with our extra supplies and we keep them in the garage. If we have to evacuate by car, it's quick and easy to grab our Go-bags, throw the extra supplies stash in the trunk of the car and we are ready to roll.

Add more food to your extra supplies stash (canned food is fine!) and by all means, pack as much water as you can. The one gallon per person per day guideline bodes well here. I'd also recommend you consider adding a little more for hygiene and sanitation purposes. Also, a portable camp stove to heat food and water would be a nice addition to your extra supplies stash.

Maintaining Your Emergency Kit

Congratulations, you're all packed! Assembling an emergency kit for your family is quite an accomplishment but it's only the first step. If you want to ensure it will come to your family's rescue during a crisis, it requires a teeny bit of maintenance. After you choose the right place to store your kit, you'll need to rotate its contents, and occasionally practice using each item.

STORING YOUR KIT

A Go-Bag for each family member plus an extra supplies stash can add up to a lot of stuff! You'll look at the pile of packs and think *where are we going to put all of this?* Then the top shelf in the garage will come to mind, in the spot next to the Christmas lights and Halloween decorations. It's seems like the perfect place—nicely out of the way—because, after all, you won't be using the emergency kit that often and hopefully never, right?

Not quite. While it's tempting to store your Go-Bags somewhere out of the way, it's not ideal. When seconds count, you will need to grab them with little or no fumbling. Choose a place where your bags will be out of sight, but still be easily accessible. A hall closet near the front door, perhaps? It's fine to store your extra supplies stash in the garage near your car since that part of your kit is designed specifically for a vehicle evacuation.

Once you've decided on a storage location for the Go-Bags, make sure everyone in the family knows where it is. And if you ever change the location, be sure to show everyone the new spot.

ROTATE YOUR SUPPLIES

Right before my husband and I became parents, we put together our first emergency kit. We packed the kit full of new baby needs and stored it in the garage. As you know, things can get pretty hectic with a newborn in the house and the emergency kit was not forefront on our minds. When we did finally remember to update it, our newborn wasn't so new anymore. Half of what we had packed would have been of no use to us. Talk about a major catastrophe!

If you want your emergency kit to come through for you in a crisis, you can't set it and forget it. It will be useless if it's stocked with expired food, medicine and items that are no longer relevant to your family's needs. The best way to keep your Go-Bag up-to-date is to set up a bi-annual maintenance schedule to review its contents. An easy way to remember: when you change your clocks, change your Go-Bag contents. Add fresh water and check the expiration dates on food and medication. Swap out the old for new if necessary and rotate your winter gear in or out.

PUT YOUR KIT TO THE TEST

All the emergency supplies in the world won't do your family any good if you don't know how to use them! Have you tried your water filter or is it sitting in the box in the bottom of your pack? Do you know how to construct a tent from a tarp and paracord? Will your solar charger still charge your phone on a day with hardly any sun? Practice with your gear now. Even if you managed to keep your wits about you in a crisis, you will have little time to read the owner's manual.

In addition to getting familiar with how the contents of your Go-Bag work, test the practicality of the bag itself. Have the whole family strap on their packs and take a nice long walk. You'll quickly see whose backpack is too heavy and where you need to make adjustments.

YOUR FAMILY EMERGENCY KIT CHECKLIST

Just as no two families are the same, no two emergency kits will be same. Before you get busy customizing your kit family's needs, be sure to include the essential supplies. **Pack these bare essentials for survival in your family's Go-Bags:**

→ SHELTER

- ❑ Fleece pullover per person
- ❑ Light-weight, long-sleeve shirt per person
- ❑ 1 pair of pants per person (these can be cut to make shorts!)
- ❑ 2 pair of socks per person
- ❑ 2 pair of underwear per person
- ❑ Sturdy walking shoes—running sneakers, work or hiking boots—per person
- ❑ Rain poncho per person
- ❑ Winter gear—hat, gloves, jacket per person
- ❑ Wide brimmed hat
- ❑ Sunglasses per person
- ❑ Bandana per person
- ❑ Work gloves
- ❑ Tarp and paracord for tent
- ❑ Sleeping bag per person

→ WATER

- ❑ 3 liters of water per person, minimum
- ❑ 3 containers—include 1 stainless steel water bottle or metal canteen to hold water
- ❑ Water filter
- ❑ Purification tablets

→ FOOD

- ❑ 3 days of no-refrigerate, no-cook, non-perishable food per person
- ❑ Hard candies or gum
- ❑ Infant needs: formula, sterile bottles, baby food

→ FIRE

- ❑ Matches in a waterproof container
- ❑ Lighters
- ❑ Fire-starter material—Wet Fire, dryer lint, or cotton balls dipped in Vaseline.

→ FIRST AID

- ❑ Sunscreen
- ❑ Insect repellant
- ❑ Lip balm
- ❑ Over-the-counter medication
- ❑ Prescription medication
- ❑ Special needs—glasses, contact lens solution, hearing aid batteries, etc.
- ❑ First aid kit
- ❑ First aid manual
- ❑ Moleskin
- ❑ Mylar emergency blanket per person
- ❑ Hand warmers

→ HYGIENE

- ❑ Toilet paper per person
- ❑ Disinfecting wipes—Clorox and WetOnes
- ❑ Hand sanitizer
- ❑ Small towel per person
- ❑ Bar of soap
- ❑ Feminine protection
- ❑ Deodorant

- ❑ Comb
- ❑ Toothbrush per person
- ❑ Toothpaste
- ❑ Small mirror
- ❑ Infant needs: diapers, baby wipes, diaper rash ointment, pacifier
- ❑ Elderly needs: bladder control supplies, denture needs

➔ TOOLS AND EMERGENCY SUPPLIES

- ❑ Pocket knife
- ❑ Multi-tool
- ❑ Can opener—just in case someone hands you canned food!
- ❑ Duct tape
- ❑ Collapsible shovel
- ❑ Zip ties
- ❑ Plastic garbage bags with twist ties
- ❑ Extra set of house and car keys
- ❑ Flashlight with extra batteries, per person
- ❑ LED headlamp with extra batteries per person
- ❑ Emergency candles
- ❑ Glowsticks
- ❑ N95 face mask per person
- ❑ Foam ear plugs per person
- ❑ Whistle
- ❑ Small notepad and pencil
- ❑ Sharpie marker
- ❑ Compass
- ❑ Maps
- ❑ Battery powered or hand crank emergency radio with extra batteries
- ❑ Cell phone
- ❑ Solar or hand crank cell phone charger
- ❑ Cash in small denominations, including coins
- ❑ Pepper spray or another form of self-defense
- ❑ Deck of cards
- ❑ Book or magazine
- ❑ Inspirational item or comfort item

These items make up your extra supplies stash. Pack them in a waterproof container of your choice and store it with your Go-Bags:

- ❑ 3 gallons of water per person, minimum
- ❑ Additional non-perishable food
- ❑ Portable camp stove with fuel
- ❑ Metal cook pot
- ❑ Metal cup per person
- ❑ Metal spork per person, or plastic utensils
- ❑ Dish detergent
- ❑ Pot scrubber
- ❑ Aluminum foil
- ❑ Ziploc bags in assorted sizes
- ❑ Plastic tablecloth
- ❑ Paper towels
- ❑ Paper plates
- ❑ Plastic cups
- ❑ Napkins
- ❑ Shaving cream
- ❑ Razor
- ❑ Mirror
- ❑ Bleach
- ❑ Plastic sheeting
- ❑ Disposable camera
- ❑ Fire extinguisher
- ❑ 5-gallon bucket with lid

SURVIVAL SAVVY **PETS**

Fido and Fluffy are relying on you to keep them safe in an emergency. Don't forget to make an emergency kit for your pets!

- ❑ Dry pet food for three days, minimum
- ❑ Water for three days, minimum
- ❑ Non-tipping bowl
- ❑ Leash, collar with identification tags and muzzle (if necessary)
- ❑ Pet carrier
- ❑ Kitty litter, small litter box and scoop
- ❑ Small blanket for scooping up scared cats or for bedding
- ❑ Pet waste bags
- ❑ Pet first aid kit
- ❑ Medications
- ❑ Copy of immunization records
- ❑ Photo of pet
- ❑ Veterinarian's name and number
- ❑ Written instructions for feeding and medications in case you need to board your pet.

WHAT SHOULD YOU PACK IN YOUR **CHILD'S GO-BAG**?

→ INFANTS AND TODDLERS (AGE 0-4)

Obviously, your baby can't carry a Go-Bag so you'll have to leave room in your pack for your littlest one's needs. **Here are some baby essentials you need to be sure to include in your Go-Bag:**

- ❑ Diapers
- ❑ Baby wipes
- ❑ Diaper rash cream
- ❑ Formula and baby food—even for breast feeding babies!
- ❑ Pre-sterile bottles
- ❑ 2 pacifiers
- ❑ Infant medication
- ❑ Infant sling or carrier
- ❑ Baby sunscreen, for infants over 6 months old
- ❑ Baby bug repellant
- ❑ 6 onesies or baby pajamas
- ❑ 2 pairs of baby socks
- ❑ Baby blanket

Preschoolers should be able to carry a backpack specifically made for toddlers if it's sized right. But it still can't be weighed down with tons of stuff, so plan on doing most of the heavy lifting. All clothing, hygiene, and medical items should go in your pack but **your toddler can help out by carrying the following items:**

- ❑ Identification—name, parents' names, address, phone, out-of-area contacts' information
- ❑ 1 liter of water in one container
- ❑ Toddler-friendly snacks—like Goldfish or Cheerios for three days
- ❑ Sippy cup
- ❑ Nighttime diapers or pull-ups and extra underwear for kids in potty-training
- ❑ Coloring book and crayons
- ❑ Stuffed animal or another comfort item

→ SCHOOL AGE KIDS (AGE 5-10)

Kids in this age group should be able to carry all items specific to them. Depending on their size though, the younger ones may still have some difficulty. Pack wisely. **Put all the items listed below in their Go-Bags then ask them to try on the packs to test out the weight.**

- ❑ Identification—name, parents' names, address, phone and out-of-area contacts' information
- ❑ 2 liters of water in 2 separate containers
- ❑ 3 days of no-refrigerate, no-cook, non-perishable food
- ❑ Hard candy or other comfort food
- ❑ Fleece pullover
- ❑ Lightweight long sleeve shirt
- ❑ Pair of pants
- ❑ 2 pairs of wool socks
- ❑ 2 pairs of underwear
- ❑ Rain poncho
- ❑ Wide brimmed hat
- ❑ Winter gear—hat, gloves or mittens, jacket (seasonal)
- ❑ Sleeping bag
- ❑ Toothbrush
- ❑ Small towel
- ❑ Flashlight
- ❑ Bandana
- ❑ Sunglasses
- ❑ N95 mask
- ❑ Jump rope
- ❑ Coloring book and crayons
- ❑ Portable video games, such as iPod Touch or DS with charger
- ❑ Stuffed animal or a few small, non-battery toys

→ TWEENS AND TEENS (AGE 11+)

Your tweens and teens can carry all the same items as the school-age children, plus an additional liter of water. Also, let them help you out. **At this age, they can share some of the responsibility for the family's load.**

CHAPTER 3

Be Ready in Your Pantry

Is your pantry ready for an emergency? Judging by how quick the store shelves are stripped bare before an approaching storm, I'd go out on a limb and say, probably not. A backup water and food supply in your pantry will **keep your family at home** rather than in line after a major disaster. It can even be handy for those months when your grocery budget comes up short.

Stock Up On Water

According to the Environmental Protection Agency, in 2008, the average American family of four used up to 400 gallons of water per day. Today, by some estimates, that number is believed to be closer to 600 gallons. Regardless of the number, there's one thing we can all agree on—water is a necessity in our daily lives.

How Much Water Should I Store?

As we discussed in the last chapter, the official emergency management advice for how much water to store is one gallon per person, per day. This amount should be enough for drinking and for some basic cooking, but when you figure in cleaning, bathing, and flushing toilets one gallon doesn't seem like enough. Then you have to factor in these considerations: Do you have pets? Are you a nursing mom or do you use water in order to prepare formula? Do you have an elderly or sick family member who needs water to take medicine or for personal care? Keep in mind pets, children, nursing moms, and chronically ill family members can increase the amount of water you need. Also, if you live in a hot climate your water requirement doubles. Once you look at the whole picture, you'll understand why I suggest you try to store closer to two gallons of water per person, per day instead.

Now, how many days worth of water should you set aside? An emergency kit is packed with a minimal three-day supply because it needs to be portable. In your home, a three-day supply is probably not enough. Looking at past disasters, you see it can take a lot longer than three days for things to get sorted out. For example, six weeks after the 2014 Elk River chemical spill—a disaster affecting up to 300,000 West Virginians—some residents were still not using water from their taps. That's why I urge you to store no less than a two-week supply in your home.

How Do I Store It?

If the average family of four stored the minimum of one gallon per person, per day, a two-week water supply would amount to 56 gallons. That's a lot of water! Luckily, there are several options for amassing your water storage—store-bought bottled water, empty soda bottles, WaterBricks and water barrels to name a few.

STORE-BOUGHT BOTTLED WATER

Store-bought bottled water wins the votes for the safest and most reliable way to secure an emergency water supply for your family. And for busy parents, it's hard to beat the convenience. One case of 24 bottles totals just over three gallons. Pick up a case or two of Dasani every time you go to the grocery store and before you know it you will have a sizeable supply. Bring home five cases and you'll have one family member's drinking needs covered for two weeks. Here's another reason to like store-bought water bottles: they are easy to store. You can stack them three-feet high in the back of a closet or tuck a two-week supply under everyone's bed.

So, what's the biggest downside to building your supply this way? Definitely, the expense. My family tries to get around it by stocking up during the Buy-One-Get-One-Free sales that run approximately every six weeks at our local grocery store. And then of course there's the waste. Water bottles are meant to be used once and recycled. If they are refilled, they lose their safe status.

EMPTY SODA BOTTLES

Empty soda bottles make a great container for storing water. Made of food safe polyethylene terephthalate (PETE) plastic, these bottles are durable, portable, easy to tuck into smaller storage spaces and best of all, free! We all know free is the way to go, but before you enlist on a bottle collecting mission there's a few things you

should know. Empty soda bottles aren't stackable so if you amass a lot of them you will need to be creative with your storage space. Also, empty soda bottles require a lot of effort on your part to clean, sanitize and fill. They also need to be rotated frequently as their shelf life isn't as long as commercially bottled water.

What kind of effort are we talking about? Before you fill a soda bottle with water, it needs to be sanitized. First, wash the inside of the bottle with hot, soapy water. Be sure to rinse it completely, taking care not to leave any residual soap inside. Next, fill the bottle with one quart tap water. Add one teaspoon of unscented household bleach and cap the bottle. Swish the mixture around inside so it touches all surfaces then pour the solution out. Give the bottle a good rinse with clean water and you are ready to fill it to the top with water from the tap.

Once the bottle is filled, you may or may not have to take one more step. If your tap water comes from an utility company that treats it with chlorine, then it doesn't need any additional treatment. If not, or if your tap water comes from a well, you will need to add two drops of bleach before you cap the bottle.

Lastly, it's a good practice to label your bottles as drinking water and don't forget to write the fill date. This will make it easier to stay organized when it comes time to rotate.

One more thing, if you are a milk or juice drinker rather than a soda fan, you may be tempted to use milk or juice jugs instead. Unfortunately, these jugs are not suitable for storing water. Left-over milk protein and juice sugars are embedded in the plastic. When you add water you create the perfect breeding ground for bacteria. A two-liter soda bottle is always the better choice for free fill-your-own water storage.

WATERBRICKS

WaterBricks are large, rectangular shape containers that hold up to 3.5 gallons of water. They are made of a food-safe plastic called high-density polyethylene (HDPE), which is more durable than PETE soda bottles. Also, WaterBricks are opaque, making it more difficult for algae to take up residence inside. Some of my family's water supply is stored in Waterbricks and I like them for two reasons: They have handles for easy toting (a big plus since one water-filled brick weighs 28 pounds) and they are stackable. Each brick has an interlocking system, similar to Legos, allowing you to stack them up to four feet high. If you'd rather not stack them, the individual containers are small enough to slide under a bed.

Like store-bought bottled water, the only downside to WaterBricks is the upfront expense. Each container from WaterBricks.com costs a little more than $17, so buying enough for a family's water supply will add up quick. But unlike store-bought bottled water, WaterBrick containers are more of an investment. The containers are reusable and have a bio-degradable shelf life of up to 15 years.

If you decide to use WaterBricks for your container, they will require the same sanitization and filling process as empty soda bottles.

WATER BARRELS

If you are lucky enough to have a large storage area, water barrels may be for you. Like WaterBricks, water barrels are made of durable, opaque HDPE plastic. Each barrel can hold up to 55 gallons of water. The downside is once the barrel is filled, it's difficult to move: one barrel weighs more than 400 pounds. And then there's the expense. Shop various emergency supply retailers, and you will see the price range from $75 to over $100 per barrel. In addition to barrel, you will also need to purchase a siphon to get water out and several smaller containers to transport water.

Choosing a Storage Location

A consistently cool location out of direct sunlight is the best place to store your water supply so that it remains safe to drink for the entire duration of its shelf life. Don't store water near gasoline, kerosene, pesticides or strong smelling cleaning solutions, especially if you are using PETE plastic, as the vapors will permeate the bottles. If your chosen location has a concrete floor, put a layer of cardboard or wood between your container and the floor. This will prevent the concrete from leeching chemicals into the containers, contaminating the water or degrading the plastic enough to cause a leak. Speaking of leaks...unfortunately, they can happen so be sure your valuables aren't stored nearby.

BE READY QUICK TIP!

If the water you are about to treat is cloudy or has particles floating in it, you will need to filter it first. Pour it through a coffee filter or a clean cloth like a bandana and into a container. Then proceed with the treatment process of your choice.

Rotate Your Storage

Yes, it's true, water never goes bad, but there's always the chance that disease causing critters may sneak in during the filling process. Over time they will contaminate your water. To ensure your family has safe, drinkable water in an emergency, it's a good idea to rotate your water supply every six to 12 months. Some emergency supply retailers sell a chemical water preserver you can add to your container before capping it and then you will only have to rotate every 5 years. The product is made to treat one gallon of water or more so it will work if you are using WaterBricks or water barrels.

If you think stocking up on store-bought bottled water is the way to avoid rotating, think again. Although, commercially bottled water doesn't expire, each bottle is stamped with a Best By date of approximately two years from the day it was bottled. After that date, the water may have a funky taste.

Emergency Water Sources

What do you do if you're in the middle of a crisis and you've gone through all of your water storage? Here's some good news for a bad situation. Every home has a built-in supply of water that is safe for drinking and a supply that is unsafe for drinking but can be used for other purposes. Plus there may be a water source outside your home.

WHAT TO DRINK

The largest source of emergency water inside your home is your hot water heater, unless you have replaced it with the newer tank-less version. If you still have the old style water heater, and it hasn't been damaged in the disaster, you can drain the tank and use the water for drinking, cooking, cleaning dishes and brushing teeth. To drain the tank, you must make sure the electricity or gas is turned off and allow time for the water inside the heater to cool. Attach a short food-safe hose to the drain at the bottom of the tank. Then shut off the valve that supplies water to the tank and open the hot water faucet in one of your sinks. When you open the drain at the bottom of the tank, you will be able to collect water. Be sure to use a clean container.

Your plumbing pipes are another source of drinkable water. After the main water supply to your home has been shut off, you can drain the remaining little bit of water out of your pipes by opening a faucet located on the highest level of your house. Then let the water flow out of another faucet in the lowest level of your home and into a container.

Don't forget the ice cubes in your refrigerator. They can be melted for clean water. Also, the liquid from any canned vegetables in your pantry can be consumed. Just note this liquid will contain a lot of sodium so you may want to cook with it rather than drink it outright.

Outside of your home, look for moving bodies of water: natural springs, rivers, streams and creeks. Ponds and lakes are also options and of course you can always collect rainwater. Remember, water from these sources will need to be treated before it's safe to drink.

WHAT NOT TO DRINK

There are a few sources in your home providing water that's unsafe to drink but still is useable. Water from a swimming pool can be used to wash clothes and flush toilets. If you have a water bed, you have even more water for flushing toilets. Some sources are completely off limits. Do not use water from toilet tanks and car radiators.

Most importantly, never drink flood water. Flood water often contains raw sewage, chemicals and other toxic substances. No matter how you treat flood water it will never be clean.

How to Treat Water

If there is any chance the water you are about to drink could be contaminated with germs or bacteria, you'll want to disinfect it or purify it to keep from getting sick. There are several ways to treat contaminated water. No way is perfect but it's most effective to use a combination of different methods to make potable water.

BOILING

Boiling is the oldest method of making water safe to drink. When you boil water you kill most, if not all, of the pathogens or bugs that make us ill. Simply put the water in a pot over a heat source, cover it with a lid and bring it to a rolling boil for a full minute. Remove the pot from your heat source and keep it covered until it cools. Sometimes after boiling, the water will taste flat. Pour it back and forth between two containers a few times for an easy aerating process that improves the taste.

BLEACH

Bleach is commonly used to treat contaminated water because it kills most of the nasty organisms. I know you're thinking, Seriously? You want me to drink bleach? And my answer is yes. Unless you drink bleach straight from the bottle or use an obscene amount to disinfect your water, it's a perfectly safe treatment method.

Not all bleach is the same, though, so be sure to use only unscented, regular household bleach containing 5.25 to 6.0 percent sodium hypochlorite. Bleach also becomes less potent starting at 6 months from the manufacture date, so use a recently purchased bottle, rather than one that's been sitting under your kitchen sink for the past two years. In fact, it's not a bad idea to replace your bottles of bleach, unopened or not, every year. This will guarantee you always have a fresh supply on hand.

To disinfect water, use an eyedropper to add eight drops of bleach per one gallon of clear water. If the water is murky or cloudy, double the amount of bleach. Cap the container and give it a shake. Let it sit for 30 minutes, then open it up and smell. If the water doesn't have a slight chlorine scent, repeat the dosage and let it stand for fifteen more minutes. If you still don't smell bleach in the water, throw it away and find water from another source.

WATER FILTRATION SYSTEMS

In the last chapter, I recommended adding a water filtration system to your emergency kit. If you followed my advice you will have one in your Go-Bag. Pull it out of your kit and use it or purchase a freestanding unit, like a Berkey system or the Katadyn Ceredyn Drip Filter made for home use. These systems are capable of filtering larger quantities of water. Keep in mind the filter elements inside all systems eventually need to be replaced so it's a good idea to have a few on hand.

Stock Up On Food

The days of overstocked storerooms are gone. In an effort to reduce waste and keep costs as low as possible, many grocery stores use a just-in-time (JIT) inventory system. A steady stream of small deliveries, arriving "just in time" replenishes their stock when supplies start to dwindle. From a business perspective, limited inventories make sense and normally, it works fine. We hop in the car, arrive at Whole Foods and find all the ingredients we need for dinner there waiting.

Now imagine for a minute something – hurricane, winter storm – prevents the trucks from making deliveries and the store shelves weren't restocked? Would it cause you to panic? Not if you had plenty of food in your pantry.

How Much Food Should I Store?

Your Go-Bag should be stocked with three days worth of food. Your home, however, should be stocked with more. In the last several years, we've actually seen some large scale disasters cause significant damage and disrupt the normal supply systems we take for granted. In these cases, three days went by and residents were still relying on outside assistance. You can prevent this from happening to your family if you have at the very minimum, a two week supply of food for your family in the house at all times. An even better goal would be enough for one month. And if storing more than that gives you peace of mind, go for it!

What Food Should I Store?

No two pantries will be the same because there's no one-size-fits-all food storage plan. You will need to customize your pantry to your family's tastes and nutritional needs; however there are some basic guidelines to help you get started.

Choose foods that are simple to prepare. Emergency food should require little to no cooking in case you are without power. Also, you should select foods that require no refrigeration for the same reason. Some examples are beans, pasta, rice, peanut butter, crackers, cereals, nuts, and trail mix. Meal replacement bars, protein powder for shakes, dried soup mixes and canned goods like meats, vegetables, fruits and soups are also good options.

Keep it simple and don't go overboard. Emergencies are not the time to be preparing a five course extravaganza for every meal. In fact, you don't even need to have a different meal every night of the week. Remember, you will only be eating this way until the disaster sorts itself out. You want just enough of a variety to meet your family's nutritional needs. Once every thing gets back to normal, by all means prepare that five course meal.

Most importantly, stock up on the foods your family likes and will eat. If no one eats SPAM in good times, they won't be eager to eat it during a crisis. On the same note, an emergency isn't the best time to introduce a new food to your loved ones. Be sure to test out your latest and greatest culinary creation on your troops beforehand.

How to Stock Your Pantry

Don't rush off to go grocery shopping without taking some time to get organized first. Go through your pantry and take stock of what you already have.

Think about the meals your family eats regularly. What breakfasts, lunches and dinners are easy to prepare and only require a few simple ingredients? Is there a meal you normally make with fresh ingredients that could just as easily be made with canned substitutions? If you're hard pressed for ideas, now's the time to experiment with different "emergency" recipes. Once you find a recipe everyone likes, incorporate it into your regular menu planning.

Choose three or four dishes for each of the three meal times—breakfast, lunch and dinner—and don't forget to include snacks. Make a list of all the ingredients in each dish. Next, figure out how many times your family will eat each meal over a two week period. Then multiply each ingredient by that number. This will tell you how much of each ingredient you need to store in your pantry.

For example, a pancake breakfast for my family requires two cups of pancake mix. If I plan on serving pancakes for breakfast six times over a two week period, I need to multiply two cups times six for a total of 12 cups. And since I know that a 32-ounce box of Aunt Jemima Original Pancake Mix contains six cups of mix, and six times two equals 12, I realize I'd better keep two boxes of Aunt Jemima in my

pantry at all times.

Compare the quantities of ingredients you need with the quantities you already have in your newly organized pantry, and then make a shopping list. Buy everything all at once during your next shopping trip or add a few items at a time over a period of several weeks. Do whatever works best for your budget!

Rotate, Rotate, Rotate!

Once you have accumulated your two-week food supply, use it. A common mistake people make is thinking of it as emergency food. They pack the food, tuck it in the back of a bedroom closet and forget it's there. Taking this approach is risky. Do you want to risk ending up with expired, unusable food when you need it most?

The best way to prevent that from happening is to add your food to your everyday pantry. Then develop a rotation system. The easiest one is known as "First in, first out". Even though most foods are stamped with an expiration date, get in the habit of re-writing the expiration dates in a more visible spot on the package. When you need an item, compare the dates, grab the oldest from the shelf first and buy a replacement the next time you're at the store.

Back to the Aunt Jemima example, I mentioned I always need two boxes of pancake mix in my pantry but I actually store three. This way I never come up short. The first and oldest box is opened and the other two sit on standby. When the first box is empty, I open the second. The third moves to the front of the shelf. Once I purchase a replacement, I mark it with the expiration date and place toward the back of the shelf.

Freeze-Dried Meals

Freeze-dried meals are a busy parents' dream come true! Entrees like pasta primavera, chili mac, beef stroganoff and chicken and rice are created from fresh food that goes through a flash freeze process. The ice is evaporated then the meal is vacuum sealed in a pouch or can. When you are ready to eat one, just add hot water to rehydrate it. Voila! You have a meal that has almost the exact same taste, smell and texture as the fresh food version. I say almost because some freeze-dried food companies offer better tasting meals than others. Always try each entree to be sure it suits every family member's taste buds before you invest in a large supply. In my family, meals from Mountain House and Legacy Foods win the taste tests every single time.

In addition to convenience, freeze-dried meals are favorable because of their extended shelf-life. Depending on the brand and packaging, entrees can last up to twenty five years. When stored at room temperature in a dry location, these meals retain their flavor and nutritional quality the entire time.

The biggest downside to freeze-dried meals is the upfront expense. Whether you purchase entrees in a #10 can or individual pouches packaged in a one-month supply kit, you are paying in advance for several servings of meals you may not eat for a long time. This can be tougher on your monthly food budget than weekly grocery shopping.

So why would I suggest you consider buying food that lasts for 25 years when you only need a supply to hold you over for two weeks minimum? There's a certain peace of mind that comes with knowing there's always a few meals tucked away in the back of your pantry that you don't need to keep track of or replenish as often.

GROCERY SHOPPING CHECKLIST

Your family's taste buds will determine which foods go on your grocery list, but don't forget to stock up on these non-food essentials:

- ❑ Aluminum foil
- ❑ Paper plates and bowls
- ❑ Paper cups
- ❑ Plastic utensils
- ❑ Paper towels
- ❑ Resealable bags
- ❑ Garbage bags
- ❑ All purpose cleaner
- ❑ Disinfecting wipes
- ❑ Bleach
- ❑ Dish soap
- ❑ Charcoal
- ❑ Batteries
- ❑ Lighters and matches
- ❑ Toilet paper
- ❑ Body soap
- ❑ Shampoo and conditioner
- ❑ Toothpaste
- ❑ Deodorant
- ❑ Razors and shaving supplies
- ❑ Feminine hygiene products
- ❑ Diapers
- ❑ Wipes
- ❑ Diaper rash cream
- ❑ Bladder control protection

THINK OUTSIDE THE BOX OF COOKIES

Just because fresh fruit and veggies won't be at your disposal during a disaster doesn't mean you have to resort to feeding your little ones junk food. Here are ten healthier pre-packaged snacks for your pantry that are both kid and parent-approved.

1. **BLUE DIAMOND ALMONDS 100-CALORIE PACKS**—Almonds are a delicious, nutritious snack and 100 calorie packs are just the right size for taking a bite out of hunger. Per serving: 80 calories; 9g fat; 3g carbohydrates; 4g protein; 2g fiber; 1g sugars (bluediamond.com)
2. **BARE FRUIT CINNAMON APPLE CHIPS**—Homegrown Washington state apples are baked into yummy, crispy chips that your kiddos will love. You'll love that they are non-GMO, 100% natural with no added sugar, preservatives or additives. Per serving: 90 calories; 0g fat; 26g carbohydrates; 0g protein; 4g fiber; 21g sugars (baresnacks.com)
3. **VAN'S GLUTEN FREE LOTS OF EVERYTHING CRACKERS**—Oats, brown rice, millet, quinoa and amaranth come together in a little cracker packed with a big flavor crunch. Available in other craveable creations, like Fire Roasted Veggie, Say Cheese and Multi-Grain and all are gluten-free! Per serving: 140 calories; 4.5g fat; 21g carbohydrates; 3g protein; 2g fiber; 3g sugars (vansfoods.com)
4. **CLIF KID Z BAR CHOCOLATE BROWNIE** —Active kids will ask for this organic, energy bar disguised as a chocolate brownie treat. No high-fructose corn syrup, hydrogenated oils, synthetic preservatives or artificial flavors are allowed in Z Bar. Only 100% chewy goodness. Per serving: 120 calories; 3.5g fat; 22g carbohydrates; 2g protein; 3g fiber; 11g sugars (clifbar.com)
5. **ANNIE'S HOMEGROWN CHEDDAR BUNNIES**—Choose bunnies over fish for a healthy snack made of certified-organic wheat flour and 100% real aged cheddar cheese. Here's an added plus: Cheddar Bunnies are the perfect size for teeny hands. Per serving: 140 calories; 6g fat; 19g carbohydrates; 3g protein; 0g fiber; 1g sugars (annies.com)

6. **LITTLE DUCK ORGANICS APPLE BANANA TINY FRUITS**—This toddler-friendly, dried fruit snack is the next best thing to fresh picked. Made from 100% all natural fruit, Tiny Fruits are dried slowly to preserve the fruit's nutrients and have no added sugars, salt, colors or preservatives. If your little one is not an apple fan, Tiny Fruits come in other flavors like Strawberry Mango, and Pineapple Mango. Per serving: 13 calories; 0g fat; 4g carbohydrates; 0g protein; 1g fiber; 3g sugars (littleduckorganics.com)

7. **GOGOSQUEEZ ORGANIC APPLESAUCE**—A yummy snack for on-the-go kids, GoGosqueeZ is made from USA grown, organic fruit with no peels, no high fructose corn syrup and no added colors or flavors. Just pure apples pureed into applesauce and packed in a resealable pouch with a built-in straw. Available in 10 different fruit flavors. Per serving: 45 calories; 0g fat; 12g carbohydrates; 0g protein; 1g fiber; 9g sugars (gogosqueez.com)

8. **BEANITOS BLACK BEAN CHIPS**—Your kids will be reaching for the bean chips rather than the potato chips once they taste Beanitos, a delicious, nutritious snack that's all natural, non-GMO, preservatives and corn-free. Per serving: 140 calories; 7g fat; 15g carbohydrates; 4g proteins; 5g fiber; 0g sugars (beanitos.com)

9. **STRETCH ISLAND FRUIT CO. FRUIT STRIPS SUMMER STRAWBERRY**—It's fruit leather made from real fruit! Non-GMO, 100% natural with no artificial additives and no added sugar, Stretch Island Fruit Co. Fruit Strips are equal to a half serving of fruit. If your kids turn their noses up at strawberries, try another one of the many flavors, such as Abundant Apricot, Harvest Grape, Mango Sunrise or Orchard Cherry. Per serving: 45 calories, 0g fat; 12g carbohydrates; 0g protein; 1g fiber; 9g sugars (stretchislandfruit.com)

10. **JUSTIN'S ALMOND BUTTER**—All natural, made with California almonds, Justin's nut butter is a smooth and creamy squeeze pack snack with enough fat to fill your kiddos up. Try one or all eight delicious flavors including, Chocolate Hazelnut Butter, Peanut and Honey Butter, or Maple Almond Butter. Per serving: 190 calories; 16g fat; 7g carbohydrates; 7g protein; 3g fiber; 2g sugars (justins.com)

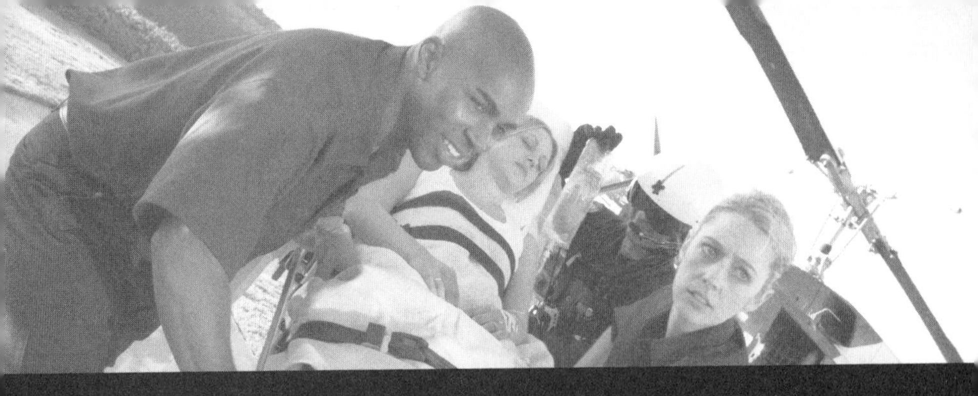

CHAPTER 4

Medical Readiness

Except for the occasional virus and scraped knee, my family had been pretty healthy so planning for a medical emergency wasn't our top priority. That changed the day I got a phone call that **my husband was in the emergency room**. Thankfully everything turned out fine but it made me realize how unprepared my family was to handle a medical crisis. No one expects to receive a bad test result, get in a car accident or be injured in a natural disaster and yet these things happen. While it's impossible to completely eliminate the stress a medical emergency causes, there are some things you can do to be ready for them which will help lessen the blow.

Build a Foundation of Good Health

The first step toward medical readiness is to do your best to prevent a health crisis. When you abuse or don't take care of your body, you're setting yourself up for all kinds of health problems including heart disease, diabetes, stroke and cancer. Here are some ways you can improve your health and at the same time be a healthy role model for your children.

EAT RIGHT

Good nutrition is important to prevent health problems like heart disease, Type 2 diabetes, high blood pressure and even some cancers. Choose fresh, unprocessed, whole foods (fruits, vegetables, whole grains, lean meats) over processed food, which lacks nutrients and fiber. Limit sugar, eat smaller portions and avoid fast food. If your family's diet needs a complete overhaul, don't feel like it has to be done in one day. Small changes over time can make a big difference when it comes to eating right.

BE ACTIVE

Studies have shown sitting for long periods of time can be just as unhealthy for you as smoking so get up and get moving! Walk the dog, take a Zumba class at the gym, sign up for a 5K or go on a family hike. To make it easier to stay motivated, find several activities you enjoy.

GET ENOUGH SLEEP

Lack of sleep increases the risk of high blood pressure, diabetes and heart disease. It also plays a role in inflammation and weight gain. While the exact number of sleeping hours a person needs depends on the individual, the recommended amount for good health is approximately eight hours for adults. Children need an average of 10 hours sleep and babies and toddlers require an additional two to three hours of naptime. To get a good night's sleep, eat your last meal two to three hours before going to bed. Turn your bedroom into a No TV-No Computer zone and create a relaxing bedtime routine. Most importantly, decide on a sleep and wake schedule and stick to it. Don't put sleep off until everything is done, instead stop doing everything and get to bed.

DEVELOP A RELATIONSHIP WITH YOUR DOCTOR

Most of us only think to go to the doctor when something goes wrong but visits when you're feeling well are important to maintain good health. Regular physical exams allow your doctor to get to know you and your family so he can give you individualized counseling based on your health history and lifestyle. Plus he'll be able to catch a health problem before it becomes serious. How often should you get a check-up? If you're healthy—a non-smoker with no disease risk factors who doesn't take prescription medication and isn't overweight—age will determine how often you should have a physical exam. Under 30 years old? Make an appointment every two or three years. If you're in the 30- to 40-year-old age range, get to the doctor every other year. Fifty and over should schedule a visit once a year. For children, always follow your pediatrician's recommendations. Infants need to see a doctor more often. As they get older, their well-checks will be scheduled further and further apart.

MANAGE STRESS

Feeling blue? Can't sleep? Have a headache that just won't go away? You're not alone. According to the American Psychological Association, more than 65% of us are experiencing physical or emotional symptoms of stress. Chronic stress increases the risk of physical health problems like heart disease, diabetes, obesity, and cancer, as well as mental health problems—depression, anxiety and more. While it's impossible to get rid of stress triggers, it is possible to manage them. Talk with friends. Meditate. Take up a hobby. Protect your time by learning how to say no.

ADOPT GOOD HEALTH HABITS

No smoking. Don't do drugs. Limit caffeine and alcohol. Drink plenty of water. Wash your hands. Wear sunscreen. Floss once a day. These are just a few of the many good health habits you can adopt to create a healthier you.

BE READY QUICK TIP!

Did you know deactivated cell phones are still able to call 911? Always remove the battery before you let your kids play with your old cell phone.

Make a Medical Emergency Plan

Medical emergencies can happen any time. Unfortunately, most of us wait until one happens before we ever think about what action we need to take. Take time now to get organized and think through the steps you would need to take if someone in your family experiences a medical crisis. A little planning beforehand will result in quick action that can make a big difference in how the emergency plays out.

Know Family Members' Medical History

Chances are you know your own medical history, but do you know your spouse's? Do you have all your children's histories committed to memory? It's difficult to remember all the details and if someone in your family has a chronic illness, things can get even more complex. A written medical history or a copy of medical records is the best way to keep everything straight. It's helpful to have when you see a doctor other than your family physician and it is vital if you have to take a trip to the emergency room.

Write down medications, conditions, surgeries and major illnesses for every person in the family. Keep a copy in your Grab-and-Go Binder (see chapter 5) and another in your car or purse. Consider making an electronic medical history called a Personal Health Plan for each member of your family. A Personal Health Plan is your web-based collection of medical records from doctors, hospitals and pharmacies. You can also add your own notes and questions to the file. These electronic files make it easy to access important medical information no matter where you are. There are several companies that provide a platform for this electronic service. Some are free and others charge a membership. To find the one that suits your family's needs, visit myPHR.com.

Know How to Call For Help

Does everyone in the family know to dial 911 for emergency assistance? Any time you call 911 for help, be ready to answer the dispatcher's questions, follow her instructions and provide her with this information:

- The street address or location you're calling from
- The phone number of the phone you're calling from
- A description of the victim's injuries or details about the symptoms the victim is experiencing.
- And if possible, call from a landline rather than a cell phone. Your landline

phone number and location is automatically captured by the emergency dispatch center which helps send medical personnel to you quickly. If you have to call from your cell phone, be sure you know your exact whereabouts because 911 operators will have a difficult time pinpointing your location.

Know When to Call 911

Call 911 when someone is experiencing a life-threatening medical emergency. Also call if you think the victim's condition will get worse while you're driving him to the hospital, if moving him will cause further injury or if traffic would keep you from getting to the hospital quickly.

Here are some signs you are dealing with a life-threatening emergency:

- Trouble breathing or not breathing at all
- Unconscious or unresponsive
- Chest pain
- Sudden intense headache
- Choking
- Severe head injury
- Difficulty speaking or slurred speech
- Sudden numbness, or weakness of any part of the body
- Sudden dizziness or mental changes, like confusion or odd behavior
- Sudden unexplained vision changes
- Uncontrollable nosebleed
- Sudden unexplained vision changes
- Bleeding that won't stop with direct pressure
- Broken bone that has penetrated the skin
- Broken leg, hip, back or neck
- Large or severe burns
- Sudden, severe allergic reaction or a reaction that is getting worse
- Extremely hot (hyperthermia) or extremely cold (hypothermia)
- Drug overdose
- Drowning
- Suicidal thoughts or threatening to kill someone
- If you think someone has swallowed, inhaled, or got poison on his or her skin and they are conscious, call the poison control center at 1-800-222-1222 immediately. If they have lost consciousness, call 911 instead.

Still unsure if your situation is a life-threatening emergency? It's better to be safe than sorry. Call 911 and let the dispatcher decide.

Know Your Way to the Hospital

Find at least two routes to the nearest hospital and commit them to memory. And it never hurts to know where the second nearest hospital is located.

Build a First Aid Kit

No medical emergency plan is complete without a well-stocked first aid kit. Having supplies on hand to treat medical emergencies—both large and small— is a must for survival-savvy families. Keep a first aid kit in your home, car, and Go Bag. Pre-made kits are available for purchase but I recommend you buy one only to use as a starting point for assembling your own. The best kits are customized to your family's needs. Your level of first aid training will be a major factor in deciding what items you should include in the kit. There's no sense having a kit filled with items you don't know how to use. Large families will have larger kits than small families. Additionally, if you have family members who have a special medical condition, your kit must support their treatment needs.

Learn First Aid Skills

Imagine for a minute, your family is sitting around the dinner table and your little one starts choking on the chicken. She can't breathe and her skin is turning blue. Now imagine no one in the family knows what to do and you all stand by helpless until the ambulance arrives. When you're facing a medical emergency, knowing what to do could be the difference between life and death. Learning basic life saving skills is critical to your family's medical readiness.

Additionally, knowing basic first aid skills could save a life in a large scale disaster. Remember how emergency management officials advise you to be able to take care of yourself for a minimum of three days? That doesn't only apply to food and water. It includes being able to handle any situation requiring medical assistance. In a disaster, first responders will be overwhelmed and it may take more time than usual for them to respond to your call for help.

TAKE A CLASS

Nothing beats the hands-on training you receive in a first aid class. It's a good idea for all the adults in your family to take a class and get certified in first aid. A class teaches you the how to respond in a medical emergency and knowing how to respond gives you the confidence to act. Visit the American Red Cross (www.redcross.org) or The American Heart Association (www.heart.org) online to find a CPR and First Aid class in your area. For more comprehensive first aid training, consider taking a two-day Wilderness First Aid course. Wilderness First Aid classes train you how to handle medical emergencies when help is not readily available. These classes are offered through organizations for outdoor enthusiasts like the National Outdoor Leadership School (www.nols.edu)

APPLY THE BASIC RULES OF FIRST AID

While the treatment will vary depending on the medical crisis, there are some first aid rules that you should follow in every situation.

→ DON'T PANIC

When faced with a medical emergency, it's easy to lose your cool. Stop, take a deep breath. Panic makes it difficult to make good decisions. Plus part of your job is to reassure the victim everything will be okay. I guarantee you won't be very convincing if you're all worked up.

→ SIZE UP THE SCENE

Before you rush to the victim's side, always check the surroundings for safety. Will you be risking your own life if you offer assistance? Remember, you won't be any help to anyone if you become injured yourself.

→ REMEMBER YOUR ABCS

Airway, Breathing, Circulation—also known as vital signs. These are the first

HOW TO TREAT A **BLOODY NOSE**

Nosebleeds are common among children and even though they look scary, most of them are more of a nuisance than a danger. Follow these steps to stop the flow:

- Have the victim tilt his head forward, not back.
- Using a clean cloth, pinch both sides of the nose together, just under the bony part.
- Apply a cold pack to the nose and cheeks.
- Hold this position for ten minutes.
- Check to see if the nose has stopped bleeding. If not, pinch it for another ten minutes.
- Most nosebleeds will stop after twenty minutes. If it continues, call 911.

things you need to check when you are administering first aid. Is the victim's airway open? Is the victim breathing? Does the victim have adequate circulation, or in other words, a pulse? If the ABCs are checked and dealt with, the victim will have a greater chance of surviving until help arrives.

→ CALL FOR HELP

If you're in the middle of a medical crisis that warrants professional emergency care, never hesitate to call 911—even when the victim says not to. Some people feel embarrassed by the attention and will tell you they are fine when they're not.

Be Ready For Medical Emergencies

This section is not meant to replace classroom first aid training. I've included it because it addresses common emergency situations. These are the first aid skills that every parent should have at the bare minimum. Do yourself and your family a favor: enroll in a basic first aid class today.

CARDIO PULMONARY RESUSCITATION OR CPR

With four out of five cardiac arrests happening at home, it's likely if you ever need to administer CPR, it will be to save the life of someone in your family. That alone should make you want to take a class and get certified in CPR.

But until you can get to a class, learn how to do Hands Only CPR. Studies have shown that chest compressions alone are as effective as full CPR—chest compressions and rescue breaths—when treating an adult in cardiac arrest. Why do you need a CPR certification then? Full CPR is still needed for cardiac emergencies involving children and infants, drowning victims, or people who collapse as a result of breathing problems.

→ HOW TO PERFORM HANDS ONLY CPR

Firmly tap the victim on the shoulder and shout, "Are you okay?" then quickly check for breathing. Watch the chest to see if it rises and falls.

If there's no response or breathing, assign the task of calling 911 to someone. Just shouting "Someone call 911!" is risky because it's easy for people to assume someone else is making the call and as a result, no one calls.

- ❑ Lay the victim flat on his back.
- ❑ Place one hand on the center of his chest.
- ❑ Place your other hand on top of the first hand, interlocking your fingers.

- ❑ Keep your arms straight, position your shoulders directly over your hands.
- ❑ Push hard and fast, at least 100 times per minute. (Oddly enough, if you push to the beat of the Bee Gees hit, "Stayin' Alive" or Queen's "Another One Bites the Dust" you'll give chest compressions at the right tempo.)
- ❑ Continue pushing hard and fast and don't stop unless one of these things happen:
  - The person starts breathing on his own.
  - Trained help arrives and takes over.
  - You're exhausted and you can't continue.
  - Your safety is at risk.

CHOKING

Choking occurs when food or another object gets lodged in the throat and prevents air from getting to the lungs. Choking is life-threatening so you need to act as quickly as possible.

→ WHAT TO LOOK FOR

- Weak cough or no sound
- Wheezing
- Grabbing the throat with one or two hands
- Panicked behavior
- Lips or skin turning from red to blue
- If the victim can make sounds or is coughing loudly, stand by and let him try to dislodge the object on his own.

→ WHAT TO DO FOR A CHOKING VICTIM

If the victim is conscious:

- ❑ Ask "Are you choking? Do you need help?"
- ❑ If the victim indicates he needs help, stand beside him and lean him forward at the waist.
- ❑ With the heel of your hand, give five back blows between the shoulder blades.
- ❑ Stand behind the victim and wrap your arms around him.
- ❑ Make a fist and place it, thumb side in, just above his belly button.
- ❑ Grab your fist with your other hand then give five quick abdominal thrusts in an upward motion.

- ❑ Continue alternating between five back blows and five abdominal thrusts until the object is forced out, the person can talk or breathe again or he passes out.

If the victim is unconscious:

- ❑ Kneel beside him and put the heel of your hand just above his belly button.
- ❑ Place the base of your other hand over the first.
- ❑ Give several upward thrusts.
- ❑ Open the mouth to check to see if the object has been dislodged and can be removed using your fingers.
- ❑ Repeat the process until the object is forced out or the victim is breathing.

→ WHAT TO DO FOR A CHOKING INFANT OR TODDLER

- ❑ Lay the child facedown on your forearm with his head in your hand.
- ❑ Using the heel of your other hand, give five back slaps between his shoulder blades.
- ❑ Check his mouth to see if the object has been dislodged.
- ❑ If it's still stuck and he's not breathing, turn the child onto his back.
- ❑ Using two fingers, give five chest compressions in the middle of his chest.
- ❑ Check his mouth to see if the object has been dislodged.
- ❑ Repeat five back slaps and five chest compressions until the object is forced out or the child is breathing.

DROWNING NEVER LOOKS LIKE IT DOES IN THE MOVIES

Yelling for help and frantically waving for a lifeguard's attention makes for a good Hollywood movie but in real life, drowning is a quiet event. Here are seven signs a swimmer is in trouble:

- The swimmer is unable to call for help.
- The swimmer can not wave for help. His arms are usually at his side and pushing down in an attempt to get his head out of the water.
- The swimmer's head is low in the water and his mouth is at water level or his head is tilted back and his mouth is open.
- The swimmer's eyes are glassy, unfocused and sometimes closed.
- The swimmer's hair may over his eyes or forehead.
- The swimmer is straight up and down in the water and not using his legs.
- The swimmer may look like he is trying to climb an invisible ladder.

BLEEDING

Bleeding can be minor or severe but in all cases, the goal is to make it stop. Always call 911 for severe bleeding as the continuous loss of blood can lead to death.

➔ WHAT TO LOOK FOR

Minor Bleeding:

- Shallow cuts, nicks and lacerations
- Scrapes
- Bleeding stops after applying ten minutes of firm, direct pressure

Severe Bleeding:

- Large amount of blood
- Spurting blood
- Bleeding that won't stop after applying ten minutes of firm, direct pressure
- Abdominal or chest wounds
- Suspected internal bleeding

➔ WHAT TO DO FOR BLEEDING

- ❑ If there is time, wash your hands with soap and water and put on latex gloves.
- ❑ Using a clean or sterile cloth, apply direct pressure. If blood soaks through, don't remove the dressing. Place more dressings on top and continue direct pressure.
- ❑ If the cut is on the arms or legs, elevate the injury to slow the flow of blood to the area.

How to treat minor bleeding:

- ❑ Once the blood flow has stopped, wash the wound with soap and clean water. Use tweezers to remove debris, if necessary.
- ❑ Apply antibiotic ointment and cover the wound with a clean bandage or dressing.
- ❑ Change bandage as needed.

How to treat severe bleeding:

- ❑ Wrap a bandage over the dressing to help hold it in place.
- ❑ Lay the victim on their back and elevate his feet—approximately 12 inches from the ground—and cover the victim with a blanket or jacket.
- ❑ Get emergency medical help immediately.

A word about tourniquets...

- ❑ Never apply a tourniquet to control bleeding unless it's a last resort to save the victim's life. Tourniquets cause permanent damage and may lead to an amputation later on.

BURNS

A burn can occur when skin comes in contact with heat, electricity or chemicals. Burns fall into three categories based on their severity: first degree burns, second degree burns or third degree burns. Depending on their size and location, most first and second degree burns are considered minor and can be treated at home. Burns more than three inches in size should be evaluated by a doctor—especially if they are located on the face, neck, hands, feet, genitalia, buttocks or major joints. If swelling from the burn may affect the ability to breathe or if more than 10% of the body is burned, treat it as a life-threatening emergency.

→ WHAT TO LOOK FOR

First Degree Burns:

- Skin is red, swollen and painful
- No blisters

Second Degree Burns:

- Skin is red, swollen and painful
- Burn may appear wet or shiny
- Blisters are present immediately or within a few hours

Third Degree Burns:

- Skin is white in appearance or charred
- Relatively painless, numb due to nerve damage

→ WHAT TO DO FOR BURNS

- ❑ Stop the burning by running cold water over the area until the pain lessons. Never use ice to cool a burn.
- ❑ Remove any jewelry or clothing near the burn before it starts to swell. If clothing is stuck to the burn, leave it.

BE READY QUICK TIP!

Do your kids spend time at Grandma's house over the summer? If you leave your children in the care of someone else, draw up a Medical Consent Form. Hospitals cannot treat non-life-threatening injuries without a parent's legal consent. By signing the form you authorize a caregiver to approve medical treatment, saving your little one the discomfort of having to wait with a broken arm until you can be reached.

- ❑ Treat minor burns—both first- and second-degree. All others, seek medical attention.

How to treat minor first-degree burns:

- ❑ Apply aloe vera gel.
- ❑ Take an over-the-counter pain reliever, like ibuprofen.

How to treat minor second-degree burns:

- ❑ Apply antibiotic ointment and loosely cover the burn with a sterile, non-stick bandage. Clean the wound and change bandage once a day.
- ❑ Keep watch for signs of infection—fever, pus, increased swelling or change in color.
- ❑ If you think an infection has started, see a doctor.

SPRAINS AND STRAINS

A sprain occurs when a ligament stretches or tears due to sudden, unaccustomed movement, like a twisted ankle. A strain, sometimes called a pulled muscle occurs when muscle tissue is overused or overextended. As a result, it stretches or tears.

→ WHAT TO LOOK FOR

Sprain:

- Pain
- Rapid swelling and sometimes bruising
- Difficulty moving the joint
- Redness and skin feels warm to the touch near the swelling

Strain:

- Pain
- Swelling
- Muscle spasms
- Limited mobility

→ WHAT TO DO FOR SPRAINS AND STRAINS

RICE—Rest, Ice, Compress, Elevate

- ❑ Rest the injury. Avoid using it as much as possible.
- ❑ Ice the injury as soon as possible. Then use a cold pack for 15 to 20 minutes, four to eight times a day.
- ❑ Compress to prevent swelling. Wrap the injury with an elastic bandage tightly, but not too tight as to cut off circulation.
- ❑ Elevate the injury above heart level to reduce pain and swelling.
- ❑ Take an over-the-counter pain reliever.
- ❑ Go to the doctor if the injury isn't improving after two or three days.

BROKEN BONES

Broken bones, called fractures, result from a fall, blow or other significant injury and are classified into two main categories: compound and simple. Compound fractures are when the bone comes through the skin whereas the skin stays intact in a simple fracture. In the case of simple fractures, it can be difficult to tell if the bone is broken without an X-ray. In all cases, broken bones need professional medical care.

→ WHAT TO LOOK FOR

- Swelling
- Bruising
- Deformity of a limb
- Intense pain that increases when injured area is touched or moved
- Loss of function
- Bleeding
- Bone sticking through the skin

→ WHAT TO DO FOR BROKEN BONES

- ❑ If you suspect a broken leg, hip, back, or neck, do not move the victim and call 911.
- ❑ Cover any wounds with sterile dressing.
- ❑ For broken arms, hands and feet use a SAM splint or make a splint to immobilize the area.
- ❑ Find a rigid, straight object, like a stick or magazine and a cloth or towel for padding.
- ❑ Pad the rigid object first, then slide it under the injured area. Do not straighten the injured limb.
- ❑ Adjust the splint so it extends beyond the injured area on either side.
- ❑ Tie or tape the splint to the injured body part.
- ❑ Apply a cold pack and seek medical attention.

HEAD INJURIES

Minor head injuries are pretty common among children and being a parent you've probably dealt with a few "goose eggs" before. But sometimes head injuries are severe and cause bruising or bleeding in the brain. In severe cases, emergency medical attention is needed right away.

→ WHAT TO LOOK FOR

- Bleeding
- Slurred speech
- Dizziness
- Drowsiness
- Nausea and vomiting
- Vision changes or pupils are unequal in size
- Ears and nose leaking blood or clear fluids
- Black eyes or bruises behind the ears
- Deformity of the skull
- Loss of consciousness

→ WHAT TO DO FOR HEAD INJURIES

Mild head injuries:

- ❑ Stop bleeding.
- ❑ Apply cold pack for twenty minutes every two to four hours.
- ❑ Give over the counter acetaminophen for pain. Never give ibuprofen or aspirin.
- ❑ Check the victim every two hours over the next twenty-four hours for alertness.
- ❑ Get to a doctor immediately if the victim becomes drowsy or irritable, loses strength in his hands or feet, vomits repeatedly, or has a worsening headache.

Severe head injuries:

- ❑ Call 911.
- ❑ Check the victim's ABCs. Perform CPR if necessary.
- ❑ Stop bleeding.
- ❑ Keep victim still.

BASIC FIRST AID KIT

Pack the following items in a waterproof container to create a basic first aid kit:

- ❑ First aid book
- ❑ Pain relievers and fever reducers—aspirin, ibuprofen, acetaminophen, naproxen
- ❑ Anti-diarrhea medicine
- ❑ Allergy medicine—antihistamines, decongestants
- ❑ Laxative
- ❑ Antacids
- ❑ Aloe vera gel
- ❑ Sterile eye wash
- ❑ Antibiotic ointment
- ❑ Hydrocortisone cream
- ❑ Povidone iodine 10% solution
- ❑ Antiseptic towelettes
- ❑ Moleskin
- ❑ Tweezers
- ❑ 12cc irrigation syringe
- ❑ Oral thermometer and disposable thermometer covers
- ❑ Small scissors
- ❑ Safety pins in assorted sizes
- ❑ N95 face masks
- ❑ Hot and cold packs
- ❑ Disposable gloves (latex or nitrile)
- ❑ First aid adhesive tape
- ❑ Athletic tape
- ❑ ACE elastic bandages
- ❑ Triangular bandages for splinting
- ❑ SAM splint
- ❑ Butterfly strip closures
- ❑ Adhesive bandages in assorted sizes
- ❑ Knuckle and fingertip adhesive bandages
- ❑ Non-stick gauze pads
- ❑ Roll gauze
- ❑ Self-adhering roll gauze
- ❑ Potassium iodine tablets
- ❑ Hand sanitizer
- ❑ Sunscreen
- ❑ Lip balm with sunscreen
- ❑ Bug repellant
- ❑ Powdered electrolyte replacement
- ❑ 30 day supply of prescription medication
- ❑ Extra special needs equipment and supplies

TRAIN YOUR KIDS TO HANDLE MEDICAL EMERGENCIES

Would your kids know what to do if they found you collapsed on the floor? None of us like to think about our kids navigating through a scary situation without our assistance, but as parents we wouldn't be doing our job if we didn't teach our kids how to deal with a medical emergency on their own. Here are a few things you can do to get your children ready to tackle a medical crisis:

TALK ABOUT 911

Start by showing your little ones how to operate all the phones in your home. Teach your kids 911 is the number they call when they need help in an emergency. Let them know an adult will answer and tell them what to do. Help them memorize your address and phone number so they can recite it to the operator. Also, be sure they understand a prank call to 911 is considered a crime in most communities and tying up the emergency phone system with non-emergency calls keeps help from getting to someone who seriously needs it. But if they call 911 by mistake, they shouldn't hang up. Instead, advise them to stay on the line and tell the dispatcher it was an error. Explain that if they hang up, emergency personnel will still be sent to make sure everything is okay.

DEFINE A MEDICAL EMERGENCY

Now that your little ones know how to dial 911, will they call when someone's not breathing and not call when someone has a skinned knee? Be sure they understand what is an emergency and what isn't. Give examples of different emergency scenarios they could encounter like someone bleeding heavily, breathing funny or not waking up. Then talk about scenarios that aren't emergencies such as scraped elbows and stubbed toes. If you have a family member with special needs, get specific with your kids about his needs so they'll be able to recognize when something is wrong.

TEACH FIRST AID SKILLS

Kids as young as 9 and 10 are capable of performing CPR but you don't have to wait until they're close to double digits to start teaching first aid. Even preschoolers can be taught basic techniques, like how to apply direct pressure. After you've taught them what you know, contact the American Red Cross. They'll be able to direct you to any youth classes in your area. Then get your kids familiar with your family's basic first aid kit. Show them where it's located and talk about the uses for each item in the kit. Keep it simple and if needed draw pictures to show what you're trying to explain.

ROLE PLAY

Practice will help your kids be ready for real life medical emergencies. Set up pretend crisis scenarios and let the children act out the parts of victim and first aider. Unplug a landline phone from the wall so your children can practice dialing 911. Assume the role of 911 operator so they can practice relaying the important information. Break out the first aid kit and have them practice applying bandages, slings and splints on each other.

FAMILY EMERGENCY PLAN: MEDICAL HISTORY

Using a pencil, fill in all sections below. Complete one form for each family member, attach immunization records and keep with your Family Emergency Plan.

Name: ______________________________

Date of Birth: ______________________________

Blood Type: ______________________________

Height: ______________________ Weight: ______________________

Primary Care Physician: ______________________________

Phone #: ______________________________

Insurance Company: ______________________________

Policy #: ______________________________

ALLERGIES (Food, Medicine, etc)	REACTION	TREATMENT

MEDICATION	DATE STARTED	PHYSICIAN	DOSE	FREQUENCY	REASON

DATE	PAST HOSPITALIZATIONS OR SURGERIES	REASON	PHYSICIAN

SPECIAL NEEDS

Main Diagnosis: ______________________________

Secondary Diagnoses: ______________________________

____

Description of Special Needs: ______________________________

____

____

____

Description of Necessary Medical Equipment (Include Type and Size): ______________

____

____

____

____

Notes: ______________________________

____

____

____

____

CHAPTER 5

Financial Readiness

Stuff happens. And unfortunately, some of it is pretty costly. New management takes over and suddenly you are **out of a job**. The test results are in and you're facing an **expensive surgery**. Or a **pipe bursts** while you are on vacation and you come home to find a swimming pool in the basement. You can lessen the impact of these unexpected events and protect your family's financial future by adopting smart money practices.

Building an emergency fund, paying off debt, saving more, stashing cash, purchasing adequate insurance coverage, writing a will and safeguarding your important papers are simple ways to be financially ready for whatever comes your way.

The Emergency Fund

An emergency fund is money you set aside in an easily accessible savings account to be used *only* in an emergency. It's not your let's-go-on-a-cruise fund or now-I-can-buy-a-flat-screen TV fund. Think of it as your bailout fund—money you can tap into if you lose your job or your car breaks down.

The first step to building an emergency fund is to figure out how much money you need. While your income and expenses will dictate how much money you should earmark for emergencies, a good rule of thumb is to set a goal of saving three to six months worth of living expenses. And during recessions, you should consider increasing your goal to six to 12 months.

Now, before you say "yeah, right" and close this book, hear me out. When you are living pay check to pay check this seems impossible, but it's not. You can do it if you start small. Set a goal of saving $1000 first. Every time you have to pull money out for an emergency, don't get discouraged. Just keep striving for that goal. You will get there eventually, I promise.

When you finally reach your goal, you'll see you can actually do it, giving you the confidence boost needed to reach the next goal that's set just a little higher. To figure out what that next goal is you will need to list all of your expenses—the ones you *have* to pay, not the Friday night pizza, smartphone or DirecTV service. Add up the numbers and multiply by three. Then subtract $1000 and there is your next goal.

Pay Off Debt

In 2012, more than half of Americans did not have an emergency fund set aside and 40% said the reason was they have too much debt.

Listen, I know what it's like to have debt. I know firsthand how hopeless it can seem. When my husband and I got married, we were in the hole with $50,000 in consumer debt plus a student loan. That's right, yikes! The first year of marriage is supposed to be a happy time but all I really remember is a whole lot of stress and non-stop thoughts like, *How will we ever pay off these bills?* Some months, it seemed like we could barely keep our heads above water and if someone suggested we build an emergency fund we would have had a good laugh. We were barely making the $1800 a month in minimum payments. Where was the money for an emergency fund supposed to come from?

Thankfully, my husband started listening to Dave Ramsey. If you don't know Dave, he's a *tell it like it is* financial guru. He's also the author of *The Total Money Makeover*. Dave helps people get out of debt all the time through a process he calls The Debt Snowball. My husband and I were so desperate we took Dave's advice and got busy with the program. It worked for us and trust me, it can work for you too.

First, you have to do the hard stuff. Cut up the credit cards, trim your expenses, take on extra jobs, sell your stuff—just prepare yourself to do whatever it takes. Then it's time to get organized. Make a list of all your debts, putting them in order of smallest payoff balance to the highest. No, interest rates don't matter, just the balances. Every month, pay the minimum payment on all your bills except for the first one on the list (The smallest payoff balance, remember?). For that one, you are going to have squeeze every last drop out of your monthly budget and come up with some extra cash. Even if it's not much, you need to find something. Put that extra money plus the required minimum toward the smallest debt. Keep doing this every month until it's paid off.

Once you've paid off the smallest

bill, cross it off the list (Feels good, doesn't it?) and move on to the next one. Combine your extra money for the month with the minimum payment *plus* the minimum payment amount for the bill you just paid off and apply it towards debt number two. Do this every month until the balance is zero. Then move onto debt number three. Now you have the minimum payments from the bills you just paid off, plus your extra money for the month to use towards paying off debt three. See how this works?

It will take commitment and some sacrifice but don't give up. You will get out from under the pile of debt eventually. And in the meantime, if an emergency comes up, you have that $1000 emergency fund you can pull from.

It took us three years to pay off our debt. Each bill we paid off gave us the motivation we needed to tackle the next one, and believe me it felt good! It also feels really good to live free of debt. We have lived without credit cards and car payments for more than 10 years and there's a reason why it's called debt-free. Free for freedom. It's so freeing you will physically feel lighter.

Spend Less, Save More

According to a study by the American Psychological Association, 75% of us rank money as the leading cause of our stress. The best way to reduce that stress is to have a savings account. More money in your emergency fund to deal with the unexpected bills, money to pay for larger purchases like a car and money to live off of after you retire. Sounds good, right?

The only way to build a savings account is to follow the old adage - Live *below your means.* In order to do that you have to adopt a lifestyle that you can realistically afford. The first step is to find out what your means are. Track your income and expenses for two or three months to see where your money goes. Ask yourself some tough questions. Should you be buying Starbucks lattes on your way to work every morning? Can you cut back on technology, like smartphones, cable, or internet? How much less can you spend on groceries? Do you really need two cars or can you get by with one? And yes, the big one: Can you really afford the house you're living in?

After you take a good hard look at ways to reduce your expenses, make a budget. Be sure to include a small amount of play money because it will be difficult to stick to the budget if you feel completely deprived. Then determine how much money you will set aside for savings. A common goal is 10% to 15% of your income. Every payday put that amount of money into a savings account first, before you pay the rest of your bills.

Once you have a plan in place, make a commitment to stop the impulse buying. Before you make a purchase, give yourself a 24-hour breather. Use the time to determine if the item is a want or a true need. Make a game out of seeing how much money you're able to save each day. Finally, realize in today's world of plenty, there will always be material temptations. Don't lose sight of your new found goal of freeing yourself from the stress-filled cycle of living paycheck to paycheck.

Keep Cash Under Your Mattress

Okay, maybe not under your mattress, but having a little cash somewhere in your home is a good idea. If the power goes out—a common occurrence in a disaster—your debit card will be nothing more than a piece of plastic. How much you keep on hand is totally up to you, however, I don't recommend you hide away your entire life savings. Just enough to ensure your family can pay for any necessities if the ATM's out of commission. Choose an amount you feel comfortable having around and the smaller the bills the better. Change may be hard to come by in a crisis. Store the money in a safe place and using a fire-proof box is not a bad idea.

Get Insured

If there's one thing we can be certain of it's things aren't always on the financial up and up. Sometimes unexpected events occur that even an emergency fund can't cover. When you buy insurance you are essentially transferring risk of a financial catastrophe from yourself to the insurance company. Insurance won't keep bad things like property damage, illness and even death from happening but it does keep the financial burden of those events from causing havoc in our lives.

Some insurance is required by law (auto and health) and some is optional. Before you commit to purchase any policy, be sure you understand what exactly you're getting. Read the fine print. If there's something you don't understand, ask your agent to explain it to you.

AUTO INSURANCE

Auto insurance is a given. If you're going to drive legally, you have to have it. Every state has set a minimum amount of insurance residents are required to carry and most likely, it won't be enough for your family. Do your homework to make sure you get the proper amount of coverage. Also, even if you've been a loyal customer since you were 16, your insurance company still may not be giving you the best rate. Be sure to shop around yearly. Sometimes switching to another company will get you a better deal. Lastly, if you have already built up a sizable emergency fund, consider going with a higher deductible. It will save you money on the monthly premiums.

HOMEOWNER'S INSURANCE

Standing in the pile of rubble you used to call home is not the best time to find out that your insurance company doesn't have your back. Standard homeowner's insurance policies cover things like fires, theft and fallen trees, not earthquakes, floods and mudslides. Check with your insurance company now, before you need it and find out what type of coverage you have. If you are not covered for all the risks that could affect your area, ask about purchasing more coverage.

Also, don't underestimate the amount of coverage you need. Yes, you might have purchased your house for $150,000, but that doesn't necessarily mean $150,000 is enough insurance. The actual cost to rebuild your home could be much higher due to new materials and higher labor costs. Consult with a real estate appraiser or local builder and find out what is the average rebuilding cost per square foot for your area. If your current insurance coverage isn't close to that amount, increase it.

Finally, if you were to make a claim, would you be guaranteed the actual cash value or the replacement cost? Actual cash value pays you based on how much an item is worth. In other words, if your five-year-old television is stolen, the insurance company will pay you the value of the TV, not what it would cost to get a new one. Replacement cost pays you based on the cost of a new item and doesn't take in to account depreciated value.

In order to ensure the claim process goes as smooth as possible, keep an inventory of your belongings. One way is to keep a written list of your valuable items along with copies of receipts or you can get organized with software like the one found at knowyourstuff.org, the Insurance Information Institute's free online inventory system. Once you've completed the inventory, keep a copy at a safe location away from home.

LIFE INSURANCE

As parents, we have responsibilities—little people who rely on us to provide for their needs. If you pass away will your spouse and your children be able to take care of themselves financially? And it's not just the breadwinner who needs to be insured. Who would take care of the children if something happens to a stay-at-home parent? Would the surviving spouse need the help of a nanny or some other form of paid childcare? What would happen if both you and your spouse die together? Will your children's guardian have enough money to care for them? Buying a life insurance policy can be the difference between leaving your loved ones in a financial lurch or on solid ground when you're no longer around.

There are two types of life insurance, whole life and term insurance. Whole life, including variable life and universal life is an investment product and insurance policy combined. The monthly premium you pay is divided. Part of it pays for insurance coverage and the other part acts like a savings account, building a cash value that has tax benefits to be used in retirement. Whole life insurance covers you for the duration of your life versus term life insurance, which covers you for a fixed period of time, usually twenty to thirty years.

Term life is straight up insurance coverage that pays a death benefit, or money to your beneficiary if you die. There's no investment side, so the money you pay into it is gone for good if you outlive the policy.

So which one should you get? It depends on who you ask. Whole life agents will sell you on the fact that the premiums you pay for a whole life policy stay the same every month for your entire life whereas term premiums remain the same for only the fixed period. After that, the term policy ends or the insurance company may raise the rate every year until it's no longer affordable and you decide to terminate it.

Most financial planners will recommend you purchase term and stay away from whole life polices. Because there's no savings aspect, monthly premiums for term life are a lot less expensive. Then they will usually advise you to take the money you save from a lower premium and invest it instead. The same planners will also point out the hefty sales commissions the whole life agent receives for selling you a policy.

Ultimately, you should ask your agent to run a whole life versus term analysis so you can make an informed decision. Also, seek their assistance with determining how much insurance you need. The final dollar figure depends on things like your current savings, your living expenses, your children's age, a mortgage and any other outstanding debts you have.

HEALTH INSURANCE

Health care costs keep rising and we all know health insurance isn't much cheaper but it only takes one major injury or illness to leave your family in a financial mess. Studies have shown the number one reason for bankruptcy filings is unpaid medical bills, not unpaid mortgages or credit card debt. Securing health insurance for your family is the best way to keep a tough situation from getting tougher.

If your employer offers health insurance coverage then shopping for your policy just got easier. If you need to secure your own health care plan, there are a few things you need to know. In 2010, a new law, The Affordable Care Act was passed and changed health insurance, as we know it. Insurance companies can no longer cancel your policy if you get sick or set up lifetime limits, meaning your coverage can't run out. Also, they are required to offer free preventative screenings (think: mammograms) and must eliminate co-pays and deductibles for annual wellness checkups. Your children can now stay on your plan until they are 26 years old and if you have a pre-existing condition, you can't be denied coverage.

Each plan must offer a minimum standard of care, called essential health benefits like maternity and newborn care, hospitalization, and prescription coverage. Those of us who aren't enrolled in programs like Medicaid or Medicare can compare and shop for plans online via the Health Insurance Marketplace at healthcare.gov. There are five levels of plans: catastrophic, bronze, silver, gold and platinum. The major difference between them is the amount the plan pays toward your total care. For example, on average a Bronze plan pays 60% of your health care costs (you would pay 40%) versus the Platinum plan that pays 90%, leaving you to pay 10%. The average cost of a mid-level plan is $328 per month, but premium tax credits and other financial assistance are available to help pay for the premiums.

One of the biggest changes stemming from the Affordable Care Act and the most controversial is every American must have health insurance or pay a tax penalty. According to healthcare.gov, if you or your dependents don't have a policy that meets the standards set by the Affordable Care Act, you will pay the higher of two penalties—2% of your yearly household income or $325 per person in 2015—and it will increase every year.

DISABILITY INSURANCE

Disability insurance is usually the last insurance on our minds. Mostly because we think we won't need it. Unfortunately, according to the Social Security Administration, there's a good chance we will. They estimate one in four 20-year olds today will become disabled before they retire.

Disability insurance insures your income. Just like other insurance, you pay a monthly premium and if you become ill or injured and can't work for several months, the insurance pays you a portion—usually 50-70%—of your income.

If you are the sole breadwinner in your family or if you're self employed, disability insurance should be a priority. And no, workman's compensation and social security isn't enough. Most long-term disabilities are due to illness and are not work-related. And while it's true that Social Security provides disability benefits, it's not easy to qualify. Plus the money you receive is minimal—the average monthly benefit in the beginning of 2014 was just over $1,100.

Before you purchase a disability policy through a private insurer, check your employee benefits. Some companies offer employer sponsored insurance, which is less expensive to buy.

Write a Will

A will is a legal document that outlines your wishes and instructions for the distribution of your personal belongings after you die. Wills are especially important for parents because they allow you to have a say in who cares for your children in the event you and your spouse pass away together.

What happens if you don't have a will? The courts will make decisions for you based on a set formula and it may not always be what you would have wanted to happen. For example, don't assume your spouse will automatically inherit everything. It's possible your assets will be divided equally between your spouse and your children. How would that be bad? Splitting your assets could cause financial and emotional difficulties for your spouse. Assets like your house may have to sold so that your spouse can pay your children their share of your estate.

Because laws vary from state to state, it's always best to seek advice from a lawyer, especially for families with significant assets. If lawyers and legal fees will prevent you from writing a will, though, consider writing it yourself with the help of sites like RocketLawyer.com or LegalZoom.com.

And while you're in the will writing mode, draw up a durable power of attorney and a living will. A durable power of attorney lets you name a trusted person to handle all your medical and financial affairs in the event you become incapacitated and can't make your own decisions. A living will, also known as an advanced healthcare directive, is a legal document that spells out exactly what your wishes are in regards to life-sustaining medical treatments, such as ventilators and feeding tubes.

Make a Grab-and-Go Binder

Becoming financially ready for the unexpected results in a lot of paperwork. What should you do with all your important documents? Most of us use some type of file folder system but I highly recommend you create a Grab-and-Go Binder instead.

A Grab-and-Go Binder is a binder that holds all your important papers in one portable spot. In the event of an emergency evacuation, it will be much easier (and quicker!) to grab one 3-ring binder than it would be to rummage through several file folders in locked desk drawer.

SERIOUSLY? **A SOCIAL MEDIA WILL?**

When I first heard of social media wills, I thought it was a joke. Then I learned many email providers and social media sites won't give family members access to a loved one's accounts after death because doing so would violate privacy laws. Suddenly, creating a social media will doesn't seem so far-fetched after all.

The first step is to choose a friend or family member to be your online executor—someone to be in charge of all your digital accounts after you pass away. Then review the privacy policies and terms of conditions of each site you use. Create a list of every online account you have. Include all log on information—email addresses, usernames, and passwords—and write down what you would like to happen to the account. Some options are close the account, memorialize it or have it managed by a family member. Next, state in writing that your chosen executor should be given a copy of your death certificate. Some websites require a copy of your death certificate before they will close your account. Finally, attach your social media will to your physical will ensuring it's accessible in the event of your passing.

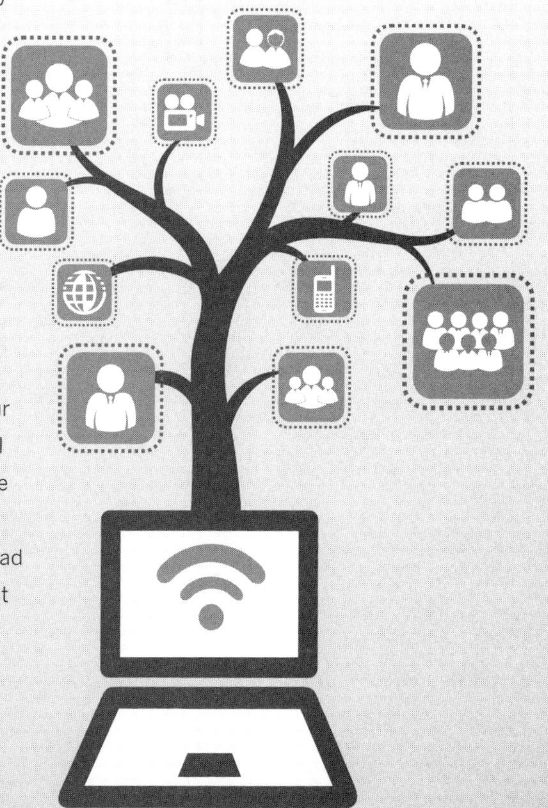

If you still can't wrap your head around this idea, at the very least be sure your spouse knows the usernames and passwords to all your accounts.

If you don't have one already, no worries. Assembling a Grab-and-Go Binder is a pretty straightforward task. Pick up three items during your next trip to Target: an 1 ½ inch 3-ring binder, a pack of clear sheet protectors and some dividers. Then, get busy organizing all your personal papers. Divide your binder into the number of sections needed to sort your documents. I created eleven categories in mine: emergency plan, auto, education, employment, family, financial, housing, insurance, life planning, medical and pets. Once your binder is finished, find a secure, yet accessible spot to store it, like a fireproof safe.

GRAB-AND-GO BINDER
IMPORTANT DOCUMENTS CHECKLIST

If you're unsure what papers to include in your Grab-and-Go Binder, use this checklist to help you get organized.

First, you'll need:

- 1 ½" 3-ring binder
- Clear sheet protectors
- 11 tab dividers

Next, label the dividers—one for each category below. Use the checklist to gather your important papers. Insert documents in sheet protectors and organize behind the corresponding divider.

1. EMERGENCY PLAN

- ❑ Completed family emergency plan

2. AUTO

- ❑ Registration and insurance card (copy)
- ❑ Loan documents
- ❑ Title/or lease agreement
- ❑ Recreational vehicle/boat titles or loan documents
- ❑ Warranty info

3. EDUCATION

- ❑ Diplomas
- ❑ Most current report card for each school age child
- ❑ Transcripts (copy) or homeschool records

4. EMPLOYMENT

- ❑ Resume
- ❑ Employment contract(s)
- ❑ Business license
- ❑ Employee benefits information

5. FAMILY

- ❑ Recent photo of each family member
- ❑ Birth, marriage, and death certificates
- ❑ Adoption records
- ❑ Divorce & child custody agreements
- ❑ Drivers license (copy)
- ❑ Military identification (copy)
- ❑ Social security card (copy)
- ❑ Passport (copy)
- ❑ Child ID kits
- ❑ Church certificates
- ❑ Military record of service
- ❑ Voter registration card (copy)
- ❑ Citizenship documents
- ❑ Concealed carry weapons permit (copy)
- ❑ Genealogy information
- ❑ List of all usernames and passwords

6. FINANCIAL

- ❑ Business cards for accountant and financial planner
- ❑ List of all banks accounts, including bank account numbers and bank phone numbers
- ❑ Copy of front and back of all credit and debit cards
- ❑ Mutual funds, annuities, money markets, brokerage account yearly statement (copy)
- ❑ IRAs, pension, 401(k), profit-sharing plan statement (copy)
- ❑ 529 plans and UGMA/UTMA statement (copy)
- ❑ Stock certificates and bonds
- ❑ Safe deposit box #, location and list of contents
- ❑ Tax return (copy)
- ❑ Student loan information
- ❑ Credit report

7. HOUSING

- ❑ Appraisal
- ❑ Mortgage statement (copy)
- ❑ Lease agreement
- ❑ Deed
- ❑ Property taxes bill (recent)
- ❑ Land survey
- ❑ Title policy
- ❑ Home inventory list—include photos/video and appraisals
- ❑ Firearm serial numbers list

8. INSURANCE

- ❑ Auto/recreational vehicles insurance policy
- ❑ Health insurance policy
- ❑ Homeowners/renters insurance policy
- ❑ Umbrella insurance policy
- ❑ Disability insurance policy
- ❑ Life insurance policy
- ❑ Long term care insurance policy
- ❑ Medicare/Medi-gap/Medicaid
- ❑ Travel insurance policy

9. LIFE PLANNING

- ❑ Business cards for attorneys
- ❑ Advanced directive, power of attorney for health care
- ❑ Authorization to consent to health care for minor
- ❑ Financial power of attorney
- ❑ Revocable living trust, family trust documents
- ❑ Will
- ❑ Final instructions
- ❑ Cemetery/funeral home prepaid fees documentation and contracts

10. MEDICAL

- ❑ Business cards for all doctors, dentists, specialists
- ❑ Health, dental, vision, prescription insurance cards (copy)
- ❑ Immunization records
- ❑ List of blood types for each family member
- ❑ Medical history for each family member
- ❑ Medical records, test results and list of prescription medication for any family member with a serious health issue

11. PETS

- ❑ Pedigree papers
- ❑ License registration
- ❑ Immunization records
- ❑ Recent photo of each pet

HOW TO RAISE MONEY-SAVVY KIDS

Do you want your child to grow up to be financially responsible? Most parents would say yes. And since few of us are financial whizzes ourselves, the thought of teaching our kids smart money practices can seem a little daunting. If you're struggling with how to start, here are seven ways to help you set your children on the path to future financial success.

1. **Get your own financial house in order.** The easiest way to teach kids how to manage money is to learn how to manage it yourself first. If you are always running up debts, paying bills late and spending on impulse, your kids will probably follow suit. Kids learn by observation and are more likely to do what you do and not do what you say. Set a good example and practice what you preach.
2. **Start early.** Research has shown that kids' money habits are formed by age 7. As long as you keep lessons simple and use terms they understand, children as young as three can grasp simple money concepts, like saving and spending.
3. **Use every opportunity to teach.** Kids are watching you earn and spend all the time. Involve them in your day-to-day finances. Talk about how much things cost and where your money comes from. Take them to the bank with you so they can see you make deposits. Giving your little ones cash at the checkout and letting them pay is a great way to teach them how to count money. When you are about to make a significant purchase, include your older children in the decision making process. And whenever you use a credit card, talk to them about the perils of plastic.
4. **Pay them.** An allowance can be an effective way to teach financial responsibility if it's structured right from the start. Determine how much will be given and then be clear about what you will and will not pay for. Set expectations for how much of the money they should save, spend and donate. It may be helpful to create a contract like the one available Money Savvy Generation (www.msgen.com). Most importantly, in order for an allowance to be a good teaching tool, you must be consistent and stick to the agreed upon schedule.

5. **Show your kids how to budget.** Budgeting is an important skill you can begin teaching at a young age. Set your little ones up with three different piggy banks—one labeled saving, one labeled donating and one labeled spending. Next, develop a budget together. For example, 20% goes to donating, 40% to saving and the remaining 40% to spending. When your children receive money as gifts or from the Tooth Fairy, help them divide it among the three banks.
6. **Don't give loans.** Kids need to learn how to live within their means. If they have overspent their allowance, don't bail them out. Let them experience the consequences of their spending choices and offer suggestions on how they can make it last until the next payday.
7. **Be positive.** There's no question, money has the ability to create stress in our lives, especially when you have a tiny voice in your ear constantly asking you to buy something. Phrase every **no** in a way that it reminds your child about choices rather than sacrifices. Instead of brushing off a request for a new toy with a brusque "We can't afford it", you might say something like "We've chosen to spend our money on swim lessons for you instead." Doing so changes their focus. Instead of obsessing about what they can't have, it teaches them to count their blessings.

CHAPTER 6

Away from Home

Busy families are always on the go. Between work, school, errands, activities, and the occasional family vacation, we spend more time away then we do at home. So what can you do to be ready for emergencies wherever you are? **Start by carrying the right supplies with you.**

Everyday Carry

Quick! Name two things you have with you every time you leave the house. That's not too difficult, right? Most of us carry a few items in our pockets or purses everyday. We tote these everyday carry items or (EDC) around in case we find ourselves in a pinch. Need some money? Pull out your wallet. Gotta make a phone call? Use your cell phone.

Now, look closely at all the items you carry. What is the purpose of each? Can you think of another use for it? For example, did you know lip balm can help start a fire? Or you can use a mirror to signal for help? Now think about what you could add to what you already carry, stuff that would be useful and reliable in an emergency. Then go about organizing your items so they're easily accessible.

Upon examining the contents of my purse, I realized just by being a mom, I had been living in a state of readiness all along. I carry the typical mom stuff—a cell phone, a wallet, keys, pens, Band-Aids, hand sanitizer, a mirror, snacks, Advil, and more. Getting organized was easy. I picked up a small makeup bag from Target and created a mini-emergency kit for my purse. I grouped together the items that weren't being used daily, like Band-Aids, and added a few other things that could come in handy in a crisis, like a small Swiss Army Knife.

The Get-Home Bag

Obviously, it isn't possible to carry a ton of life saving essentials on your person or in your purse. That's why assembling a Get-Home Bag is the next step to being ready away from home.

A Get-Home Bag is exactly what the name suggests. It's a bag of essential emergency supplies and its sole purpose is to get you home in the event of a disaster. A Get-Home Bag should be lightweight, easy-to-carry (think: backpack) and traveling with you at all times.

If you're thinking that sounds like a Go Bag, you're right. Get-Home Bags are similar to Go Bags. They are portable and they contain life saving supplies customized to your needs. However, it's their size and purpose that makes them different. Remember, Go Bags are packed with enough supplies to support you for 72 hours. And as the portable portion of your family emergency kit, a Go Bag's job is be your home base during an evacuation. Get-Home Bags are smaller than Go Bags and are meant for your car or your office. The supplies you include in a Get-Home Bag are chosen based on how far from home you regularly travel and how long it would take you to walk that distance. For example, as a mom who works from home, I'm usually no further than ten to 15 miles from the house. So there's really no need for a three-day food supply or a sleeping bag in my Get-Home Bag. On the other hand, my husband's Get-Home Bag is more substantial as his job requires him to travel 50 miles or more depending on the day.

BE READY QUICK TIP!

If you see water crossing the road, stop! Turn around. More than half of flood-related deaths result from drivers attempting to get through the water. Just 12 inches of moving water can float your car and two feet can easily sweep you away. Think it doesn't look too deep? Still turn around. You can't get an accurate read on depth. Flood waters rise quickly and in some cases the road is washed away.

Be Ready in Your Car

We've all heard stories about a driver who gets stranded in the desert and a week goes by before he's found. And maybe you share the same thoughts I used to have. Not a problem. I don't drive through the middle of nowhere. But you don't have to travel through remote areas to get stuck in a vehicle emergency. Case in point, look at all the people who spent the night on an Atlanta interstate during a freak January snowstorm in 2014. With all the time we spend driving, it's only wise take the following steps to make sure our vehicles are ready for the unexpected.

EQUIP YOUR CAR WITH EMERGENCY SUPPLIES

In addition to your Get Home Bag, every car should be equipped with basic emergency supplies meant to handle roadside emergencies. Even though roadside assistance plans like AAA are smart to have, you shouldn't rely on them as your only plan. As the saying goes, "two is one and one is none." Always have a backup.

HALF FULL IS YOUR NEW EMPTY

Running out of gas is never convenient. That alone should motivate you to get in the habit of refueling when the gas gauge reaches the half-full mark. But if you're still not convinced, here are three more reasons. One, in extreme winter weather, moisture in the air causes condensation in near-empty tanks. As a result the fuel line may freeze up and prevent your car from starting. Two, gas pumps rely on electricity so during a blackout you won't be able to refuel. And three, do you really want to be waiting for hours in gas lines after a natural disaster? Probably not.

KEEP YOUR VEHICLE IN TIP TOP SHAPE

To be sure your car will run smoothly when you need it most, stay current with maintenance. And maintenance means more than just oil changes. Get to know your owner's manual. You don't need to be a mechanic to check your car's tire pressure and treads, fluid levels, cable connections, lights, windshield wipers and battery. Then find a good mechanic and follow the recommended maintenance schedule outlined in your manual.

LEARN HOW TO CHANGE A TIRE

As I said earlier, roadside assistance is smart to have but it's even smarter to learn how to change a tire yourself. While you're at it, learn how to jump start your car and how to put on tire chains. You never know when you might be in a situation where help isn't available and these skills will come in handy.

TAKE SAFETY SERIOUSLY!

Click it or ticket. Don't drink and drive. And the latest, Don't text and drive. I know you've heard the campaign messages but are you heeding their advice? Do you keep your cars doors locked at all times, even when you're in the car? Does your baby or toddler ride in the appropriate car seat? Following simple safety precautions are the best way to keep your family safe while on the road.

Q: WHAT DO I DO IF I'M **IN THE CAR** WHEN A DISASTER STRIKES?

A: If conditions make driving too difficult, pull off the road, set the car's parking brake and wait until it's safe to travel. Turn on your radio to get the latest emergency information. Head home as soon as possible. As you drive, look for potential hazards. Stay off bridges and avoid overpasses. Watch for fallen trees and downed power lines. If a power line falls on your car, don't get out. Wait for help to arrive.

Be Ready at Work

When you're not at home, where are you? For most of us, the answer is at work. Being ready at work is like being ready at home. You need a kit and a plan.

WORKPLACE EMERGENCY KIT

For your kit, you have two options. Carry your Get Home Bag in and out of work every day or stash some supplies in a desk drawer, cubby or locker. At the very minimum an office emergency kit should include protein bars, water, a flashlight, N95 masks, a first aid kit (if your workplace doesn't already have one), an emergency radio, and a sturdy pair of walking shoes.

EMERGENCY PLAN AT WORK

If you remember, the first part of making a plan is to do your research. Do you know what disaster risks your workplace faces? Where you work will largely determine the type of emergency plan you need. An emergency response plan for workers in a high rise building will differ from the plan a construction site employee needs. Ask your employer about site specific emergency response plans and then get familiar with them. If your workplace doesn't have a plan, volunteer to help create one.

Be Ready at School

There's a certain level of trust you have to have when you send your child to school. You count on the teachers to keep your child safe in your absence. Even though most teachers do a good job, there's some thing you can do to ensure your child has the best chance of navigating through a crisis without your help. Make sure your child has the right supplies and the school has an emergency plan.

SCHOOL EMERGENCY KIT

Your child's school may ask you to assemble and send in an emergency kit at the start of the school year. The kits are kept together in a designated emergency bin in each classroom and returned at the end of the year. If the school doesn't require your child to have a kit, I recommend you make one anyways.

In the event a situation keeps you separated, an emergency kit packed with basic emergency supplies will take care of your child's needs until you are reunited. Consider school rules as you gather supplies. For example, a pocketknife is probably not the best choice. Pack everything in a 1 gallon Ziploc bag so that it will easily fit in a locker, desk or backpack. Don't forget to include an emergency information card. Even though the school has the information on file, write your name and phone number and the name and phone number of everyone who has permission to pick up your child on one side of an index card. Also write the out-of-area contacts and meeting places designated in your family emergency plan. On the back of the card, describe any health issues your child has and give instructions on how to administer medication. Because schools have strict rules against kids having unsupervised access to medication, ask the school nurse or your child's teacher to store a supply of the medicine. After the kit is assembled, talk to your child about how and when to use it.

ASK ABOUT EMERGENCY PLANS

Unfortunately, there is no standard emergency response plan for schools and daycare centers. Plans will vary depending on state laws, the school's size, available resources and the perceived risks for the area. Basically, some schools have more comprehensive plans than others and some do a better job at communicating their plans to parents.

If you're unable to locate information online regarding the school's emergency plan—including procedures and drills—ask an administrator for details. What scenarios has the school planned for? What type of drills are conducted and how often? How will the school communicate with you in a crisis? What's the shelter-in-place and evacuation plan? Does the school have supplies for an extended lockdown? What kind of training is required of the teachers and administrators? How often are the plans revised? What is expected of you in emergency?

Once you know the procedures, quiz your kids. What are they supposed to do if there's a fire? How about a tornado or a lockdown emergency? What should they do if Mom and Dad can't get to the school? Remind them regularly, it's important to obey their teacher in a crisis.

Q: HOW DO I HELP MY KIDS BE READY FOR SCHOOL DRILLS WITHOUT SCARING THEM?

A: Sometimes when you don't know what to say, it's tempting to say nothing. But not talking about potentially frightening topics won't relieve a child's anxiety. And be sure to check your own anxiety at the door before you have a discussion. Kids can sense how you feel and the vibe they get from you determines whether or not they believe your words. Be calm, confident and competent and you will teach your children to be calm, confident and competent.

Talk with your kids about the types of drills they may have at school and why they have them. Be sure to select your words carefully. Don't be too vague but don't be overly dramatic either. Make sure they understand just because the school has a plan to handle an emergency scenario doesn't mean it definitely will happen. Point out the things your kids do to stay safe everyday, like wear seat belts in the car or helmets on a bike. Emphasize that like those safety precautions, the action they take during a drill is to keep them safe and practicing helps them to remember what to do just in case.

Then, listen to your children. Find out what teachers and friends have told them about each drill. Clear up any misconceptions. Also, ask about what they are feeling. When they tell you about their fears, acknowledge them. Avoid saying things like "you don't need to feel that way." Instead you might say something like, "It's okay to feel this way." Then remind your children of the safety measures the school has in place.

And since you can't be there, always let the teachers know about your children's anxiety, so they can coach your kids through the drill experience.

Be Ready on Vacation

Unfortunately, emergencies don't take vacations. They can happen any time any where, even during your fun-filled holiday. Whether you are taking a short day-trip or a week long tour, the right supplies and a little planning could make a huge difference in how your family fares if your getaway goes bad.

PACK A TRAVEL SIZE EMERGENCY KIT

No matter where you are going or how you'll get there, never leave for a trip without a travel size emergency kit. Your kit should include the basic emergency essentials, extra supplies, copies of important documents and for peace of mind, consider adding a hotel security gadget.

→ BASIC EMERGENCY ESSENTIALS

If you're traveling by car, your Get- Home Bag will have your basic emergency supplies covered. Depending on travel distance and number of people, you may need to pack more supplies. For other methods of travel be sure to pack a flashlight, a mini first aid kit, a solar or battery powered cell phone charger, a list of emergency contact phone numbers, meal replacement bars, water, water purification tablets and a portable water filter.

→ EXTRA SUPPLIES

If someone in your family takes prescription medicine bring extra medication. And if you're traveling with a baby, pack extra baby formula and supplies. Be sure to keep prescription medicine on you and not in your luggage, especially if traveling by air.

→ COPIES OF IMPORTANT DOCUMENTS

Make a copy of your driver's license, the front and back of credit cards and health insurance cards. If you're traveling out of the country, make a copy of your passport. If your wallet gets stolen, it will be easier to cancel credit cards and issue replacements of your identification if you have the information. Unless you're vacationing at a remote location, scan the copies and email the files to yourself so you don't have to carry the confidential paperwork around with you. If you needed access to the files, you can get on the internet and retrieve them. For extra backup, it's also not a bad idea to leave paper copies behind with a friend or family member.

→ HOTEL SECURITY GADGETS

If you plan on staying in a hotel, you can beef up the security in your room with a variety of gadgets, such as portable alarms and door locks, personal safes and laptop locks. I'm a fan of door wedge alarms, like SABRE's Gatekeeper Door Stop Alarm (www.sabrered.com). The wedge slides under the door, making it more difficult to open from the outside. It also has an 120 decibel alarm that sounds when it's moved to alert you of a possible intruder.

BEFORE YOU LEAVE

When you're in vacation planning mode, research your destination. In between searching for the best kid-friendly restaurants and making reservations to swim with dolphins, get familiar with potential hazards for the area. Is your vacation spot prone to natural disasters, like earthquakes in California, hurricanes in the Caribbean or wildfires in Florida? Once you've determined the risks, it doesn't hurt to ask the hotel you're staying at what plans they have in place should an event occur.

Ninety nine percent of the time, GPS will get you where you want to go, however it's a good idea to familiarize yourself with the route beforehand just in case you hear the dreaded "recalculating". If you don't already have one, buy a map of the area your family is visiting. Mark the location of the hotel in relation to any special attractions your family wants to see and also make note of the nearest hospital.

KEEP YOUR FAMILY **SAFE AT A HOTEL**

Here are 10 ways to stay safe in your home away from home:

1. **Stay at safe hotels.**

   Does the hotel have fire alarms and an automatic sprinkler system? Hotels in the United States are required by law to have them but hotels in other countries don't necessary have to adhere to similar strict fire safety standards. Before you make your reservations, ask about the hotel's fire systems as well as the security measures such as electronic key card locks on the doors. Also, read other travelers' reviews on sites like TripAdvisor.com.

2. **Talk to your children about hotel crime and fire safety.**

   You're about to start a fun family vacation and the last thing you want to be is Debbie Downer, bringing up all the things that could go wrong. Trust me, you have to. My family woke up to a fire alarm once during a hotel stay. If we had talked about what to do prior to the actual emergency, my daughters may have been a little less panicked. And I don't even want to think about what would've happened if we had somehow gotten separated during the evacuation. The bottom line is you need to have a discussion with your kids about hotel safety before you go on vacation.

3. **Remember to pack a flashlight.**

   A fire can knockout the hotel's electrical system and you might have to navigate hallways in the dark. Keep a flashlight handy or at the very least, download a flashlight app on your smartphone. Before you go to bed, put it on the nightstand so that it's easily accessible if there is an emergency.

4. **Never publicize your room number.**

   You never know who is listening. The front desk staff at a quality hotel knows this and will hand you a room key in an envelope with the room number written on it. If your room number is announced at check-in or at any other time, always request another room.

5. **Locate the two nearest stairwell exits before you enter your room.**

   Review the map on the back of the door and locate two stairway exits near your room. If there isn't an evacuation map posted in your room, request one from the front desk. Then walk the route to the exits. Count how many doors you pass on the way there. Make a mental note of landmarks—such as trash cans, or vending machines. In the event you have to crawl through a hallway filled with smoke, the doors and landmarks will help guide you to safety. Finally, try each exit door and make sure it's unlocked.

6. **Decide on a family meeting place outdoors.**

   Just like at home, your family may not be together in a crisis. Imagine the panic you'd feel if your spouse was at a meeting in the conference room and your teenagers were hanging out at the pool when the fire alarm sounded and you couldn't find them in the chaos. Always agree on a family meeting spot during check in.

7. **Keep your doors locked and closed.**

   Whenever you are in your room, secure the deadbolt and door chain. Always keep the balcony door and windows locked. If you leave your room even for a second, take your hotel key with you instead of propping open the door. If someone knocks, never open the door without verifying his or her identity through the peephole first. If the person standing on the other side of the door isn't a hotel employee, always communicate through the closed door.

8. **Never leave your valuables in the room.**

   Nothing is considered safe in your room when you're not there. Take your iPads, wallet, and jewelry with you when you leave. Housekeeping may be trustworthy but when the door's open during room cleaning, it's too easy for a nicely dressed thief to enter the room and leave with your laptop without the maid noticing.

9. **Keep your keys wallet, and shoes next to the bed at night.**

   Every night before bed, put your room key, car keys and wallet on the nightstand. Place your shoes on the floor next to the bed. If the fire alarm sounds in the middle of the night, everything you need will be within arm's reach.

10. **Don't rush out the door if you hear a fire alarm.**

    You hear a fire alarm and your first instinct is to get out the door. Sometimes that door is the only protection you have against smoke and fire, and opening it could put you in more danger. Always feel the door before you open it. Use the back of your hand to keep from burning your palm, which will make your hand unusable. If the door is hot to touch, don't open it. Place wet towels on the floor against the door to prevent smoke from entering the room. Then call 911 and give the operator your room number. If necessary, don't hesitate to break the window.

Also, before you leave, create an emergency communications plan. How will everyone find each another if Dad's on the 12th hole of the golf course and the kids are exploring the boardwalk when disaster strikes? Decide on a safe place to meet and make sure everyone knows how to get there. Also, make sure all responsible family members have the out-of-area contact's information with them. And yes, vacations are for getting away but let someone back home know of your trip itinerary, including an alternative way to contact you in case cell phone service is spotty at your destination.

If your vacation includes a lengthy road trip, be sure your car is ready to roll. Can't remember the last time you had your car serviced? Take it in for a tune up before you hit the road. If you've been following the manufacturer's recommended service schedule, your car should be fine but it still doesn't hurt to have a qualified mechanic check the tires, fluid levels, battery, belts, lights, and air conditioning.

On the day of the trip, empty your wallet of all non-essentials except for identification, medical information and the credit cards you plan to use on the trip. Remove any spare keys from their hiding spots outside, be sure you stopped the newspaper and mail delivery, set a few lights on timers and lock all windows and doors. Lastly, turn on the alarm system as you head out the door.

DURING YOUR TRIP

Last summer, my husband and I spent a week at a California hotel. It turns out our hotel was in a tsunami hazard zone, evident by the number of tsunami evacuation route signs we saw. If you're staying in an area known for a specific natural disaster risk, take a minute to formulate a disaster plan. In our case, we followed the signs to get a better idea of our escape route then grabbed some lunch and did a little sightseeing in the "safe" zone.

Unfortunately, tourists are often targets for criminals. Do your best to blend in with the locals, including your style of dress and behavior. Ask the front desk staff at your hotel if there are any areas of town you should avoid. Leave valuables like cash or jewelry in the hotel safe. And when you do go sightseeing, don't wander aimlessly. Always have a destination in mind before you head out the door.

As tempting as it is to unplug from the world on your vacation, keep on top of the news to stay informed of any situations brewing that could affect your trip. Turn on the news channel for 15 minutes each day or catch a glimpse of the morning paper during the breakfast buffet.

GOING INTERNATIONAL?

If you're traveling abroad, there are few extra steps you'll want to take to prepare for a safe trip. Start by enrolling in the State Department's Smart Traveler Enrollment Program (STEP) at step.state.gov. This free services lets you register information about your overseas trip, including your contact information and travel itinerary. In the event of an emergency, the US Embassy will be able to contact you. You will also receive travel alerts and warnings for all the countries on your itinerary. Also visit USEmbassy.gov for the contact information and location of the US embassy in the countries you plan to visit. You'll find country specific information on local laws, types of crime you need to be aware of and the 911 equivalent for calling for emergency help.

Most health insurance providers don't cover medical emergencies overseas so consider buying travel insurance. Not only does it cover medical expenses if you get sick or injured on vacation, it also covers lost or stolen items. If your flight gets cancelled or an international crisis forces you to leave early, the policy reimburses you.

Also consider using prepaid currency cards, like Travelex or Visa TravelMoney in addition to your credit cards. Currency cards are the modern day traveler's cheques. They aren't tied to your bank account even though they act like a debit card. Also, currency cards can be replaced quickly if lost or stolen, often in 24 hours. The downside is there are fees involved—activation, reloading and ATM withdrawal fees so they can be more expensive to use than traditional debit cards.

It's A Vacation Emergency! Now What?

Whether it's a natural disaster, civil unrest, or a crippled cruise ship, if you find yourself in the middle of a crisis during vacation, follow the local officials' instructions. Then make getting home your priority. Pack up the family and as soon as it's safe to travel, and hit the road. If you are traveling by air, call your travel agent or the airlines and book a return flight as soon as possible.

While you wait for safe passage, try not to panic. Stay informed of any developments and do your best to contact your out-of-area contacts to let them know your family is okay.

GET-HOME BAG CHECKLIST

Your Get-Home Bag should be customized to your needs. Here are some suggested items to include in your pack:

- ❑ Wide brimmed hat
- ❑ Sunglasses
- ❑ Change of clothes (season appropriate)
- ❑ Sunscreen
- ❑ Insect repellant
- ❑ Hand sanitizer
- ❑ Flashlight or head lamp
- ❑ First aid kit
- ❑ Cash ($50-100 in small denominations)
- ❑ Rain poncho
- ❑ Knife
- ❑ Multi-tool
- ❑ Whistle
- ❑ N95 masks
- ❑ Small notepad and pencil
- ❑ Work gloves
- ❑ Sturdy walking shoes—running sneakers, work or hiking boots
- ❑ 2 pairs of wool socks
- ❑ 2 lighters and a set of waterproof matches in water proof container
- ❑ 1 construction grade trash bag
- ❑ Paracord
- ❑ Mylar emergency blanket
- ❑ Duct tape
- ❑ Liter of water
- ❑ Stainless steel water bottle
- ❑ Portable water purifier—like Lifestraw
- ❑ Protein meal replacement bars
- ❑ Toilet paper
- ❑ Maps
- ❑ Compass
- ❑ Pepper spray or another form of self-defense
- ❑ Battery powered or hand crank emergency radio with extra batteries
- ❑ Solar or hand crank cell phone charger

SCHOOL EMERGENCY KIT CHECKLIST

Here are some items you may want to include in your child's school emergency kit:

- ❑ Flashlight
- ❑ Small first aid kit
- ❑ Hand sanitizer
- ❑ Chapstick
- ❑ Non-perishable snacks
- ❑ Water bottle
- ❑ Mylar emergency blanket
- ❑ Comfort item—small stuffed animal, a note from you or a family photo.
- ❑ Cell phone
- ❑ Battery powered cell phone charger
- ❑ Change of clothes
- ❑ Emergency information card
- ❑ Sanitizing wipes, like Wet Ones
- ❑ Hand warmers
- ❑ Small toy
- ❑ Rain poncho
- ❑ Medication (Give to the teacher to store.)

STOCK YOUR CAR WITH EMERGENCY SUPPLIES

Be ready in your car with the following items:

- ❑ Jumper cables
- ❑ Spare fuses
- ❑ Foam tire sealant (aka Fix a Flat)
- ❑ Jack
- ❑ Spare tire
- ❑ Tire chains
- ❑ Tow strap
- ❑ Cat litter for traction incase you get stuck
- ❑ Collapsible shovel
- ❑ Flares
- ❑ Ice scraper
- ❑ Battery powered cell phone charger with spare batteries
- ❑ Flashlight
- ❑ Duct tape
- ❑ Paper towels
- ❑ Toilet paper
- ❑ 1 gallon of water
- ❑ Nonperishable food
- ❑ Lighter
- ❑ Blanket
- ❑ Tools
- ❑ First aid kit
- ❑ AAA card

CHAPTER 7

Power Outages

Power outages can happen to you regardless of where you live. And over the last several years they've been happening more often. Ice storms, tornadoes, hurricanes, lightning, heat waves, utility company problems, car accidents, and even small animals can cause a power failure. A few hours of no electricity can be fun but a few weeks without it is definitely a drag. That's why you'll want to plan ahead and be ready for **when the lights go out.**

Be Ready with a Power Outage Kit

A power outage is less of a hassle if you have a supply of powerless backups for your everyday needs—such as lighting, cooking, heating, and cooling. Some of the supplies you'll need for power outages—flashlights, an emergency radio, lighters and matches—will already be in your emergency kit. You can choose to use them or you can buy duplicates and make another kit. In my house, we keep power outage supplies in a bedroom closet separate from our family emergency kit. I'm not organized enough to keep track of who takes what out of the Go Bags. Keeping them separate is my guarantee we'll always have all the items we need if we are forced to evacuate.

Before a Power Outage

There are things you can do today while you still have electricity to help you be ready for a power outage.

Learn how to use the manual release for your automatic garage door so your car never gets trapped inside. Drive to a gas station and fill up your tank. Remember, half full is the new empty.

If you're not using surge protectors for your computer and electronics, head to the store and get some. Surge protectors are the best way to protect sensitive equipment from power spikes. Also, cordless phones won't work in a blackout so if you don't have a cell phone, be sure to buy a corded phone to use as a backup.

Bank ATMs rely on electricity so accessing your bank account may be difficult. Stop at the bank and withdraw some cash to keep in a safe place.

Once you're back home, make a list of everything you use electricity for in the house—such as lighting, cooking, heating and cooling. Then come up with a plan for how you will adapt without it.

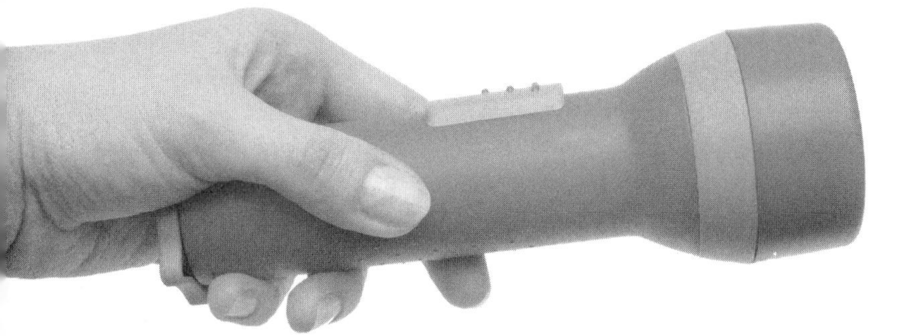

HOW TO LIGHT YOUR HOME

No need to fumble around in the dark when there are these emergency lighting options to choose from.

→ DAYLIGHT

Take advantage of the sun. During the day, open all the curtains and blinds to let in the light. Plan your schedule so most of your work or chores are done during daylight hours.

→ FLASHLIGHTS

A flashlight is the first thing most of us think to reach for when the power goes out. Flashlights are available in a variety of sizes and with the invention of the LED (light emitting diode) bulb, today's flashlights are brighter than the flashlights of yesterday. Store a flashlight in several locations around the house and preferably one in each bedroom. If you're in an upstairs bedroom when the lights go out, it will be difficult to make your way to the downstairs laundry room in the pitch dark to retrieve them. Flashlights are great for navigating through the dark however you'll find it's difficult to do stuff that requires two hands. That's why I chose to purchase a headlamp—a flashlight worn on your head—for each member of my family. And remember, flashlights are only good if they have batteries to power them so be sure to stock an extra supply.

→ CANDLES

Candles are an inexpensive light source but they can also be a fire hazard if you don't use common sense. Don't leave them unattended, don't put them near anything that could catch fire, and keep them away from kids and pets. Tea lights or votive candles in a jar are a safer option than open flame candles.

→ BATTERY POWERED LIGHTS

There's no shortage of battery powered light choices on the market today. LED lanterns by camping gear outfitters, as well as lanterns by battery manufacturers are rugged, safe and bright. You can also use inexpensive tap lights, typically used to illuminate stairwells and closets. Place them in some strategic places for a little extra illumination.

→ SOLAR POWERED LIGHTS

Solar powered lanterns have built in solar panels that charge an internal battery

BE READY QUICK TIP!

Do you always enter your house through the garage door? Automatic garage doors won't work in a power outage. Don't get locked out! Carry a house key with you at all times.

which powers the light. During the day, leave the lantern outside to recharge and at night bring it inside for light. Many solar lanterns can be fully charged via a USB adapter in advance of a power outage.

You can also buy several inexpensive pathway solar lights from your local home improvement store for everyday use in the yard. When a power failure occurs, bring several lights inside to illuminate a room.

→ GLOWSTICKS

Popular at Halloween, glowsticks are plastic tubes containing two chemicals. When the tube is bent or "cracked" the chemicals mix together and emit a luminescent glow that lasts for hours. Think of glowsticks as supplemental lighting and not your primary source of illumination as they are the least bright of all the options.

HOW TO COOK

If peanut butter and crackers for breakfast, lunch and dinner don't excite you, consider purchasing one of these powerless cooking options.

→ GAS COOKTOP

If you have a gas stove in your kitchen, the cooktop will still work unless the gas lines were damaged. Electricity powers the ignition switch so you'll need a match or lighter to light it manually. Unfortunately, you're limited to cooktop meals during a blackout. Gas ovens have safety features that don't allow you to manually bypass the lighting controls.

→ BARBEQUE GRILLS

Chances are you're already familiar with how to use a grill. At my house, we cook dinner on a gas grill more than once a week, so it would be our first choice for powerless cooking. If a gas or charcoal grill is your go-to, blackout-cooking backup, be sure you keep an extra propane cylinder or charcoal handy.

→ FIRE

If you have a fire pit in your backyard, cooking over an open fire is an option. You'll need wood for fuel, a stick for roasting food, and a metal grate to hold pots and pans. I recommend you experiment with this option before a power down emergency and learn to how to maintain heat control so you don't end up with a burnt dinner.

→ CAMP STOVES

Visit any outdoor retailer and you'll see there is no shortage of camping stoves options. Choose from single burner stoves made to fit in a hiker's backpack to larger two burner models that resemble your kitchen cooktop. Be sure to stock up on the specific fuel your camp stove requires. In a long-term power outage, you'll go through it quickly.

→ ROCKET STOVES

Rocket stoves are portable, combustion chambers designed to burn biomass, like pine cones, twigs and sticks. Producing less smoke and using less fuel than an open fire, rocket stoves are a cleaner and more efficient powerless cooking option. Fuel goes in the bottom and food goes on top. As the biomass burns, it sends heat straight up the chamber and cooks your meal. You can build your own rocket stove with the help of one of many online plans and tutorials or purchase a ready-made stove from companies like EcoZoom and StoveTec.

→ SOLAR OVENS

As long as you have sun, you can cook in a solar oven. These appliances convert sunlight into heat to roast, bake, steam or boil your food. The original, box-like All American Sun Oven is the closest to your kitchen oven. With temperatures reaching up to 400°F, it bakes bread, roasts chicken, and heats up casseroles in dark-coated pans. The new, extremely portable GoSun acts more like a grill. Place meat or veggies on the tray then insert in the glass tube chamber. In full sun, your goodies will be sizzled to perfection in less than forty minutes.

HOW TO KEEP FOOD COOL

There are a few steps you can take before a power outage to give your perishable food the best chance of surviving the big thaw.

The proper temperature for a refrigerator is at or below 40° F and your freezer should be 0° or colder. Get an appliance thermometer for both the refrigerator and freezer so you can keep tabs on any temperature fluctuations. If you think there's a chance of losing power, set your refrigerator and freezer to their lowest settings to build up a cooling reserve.

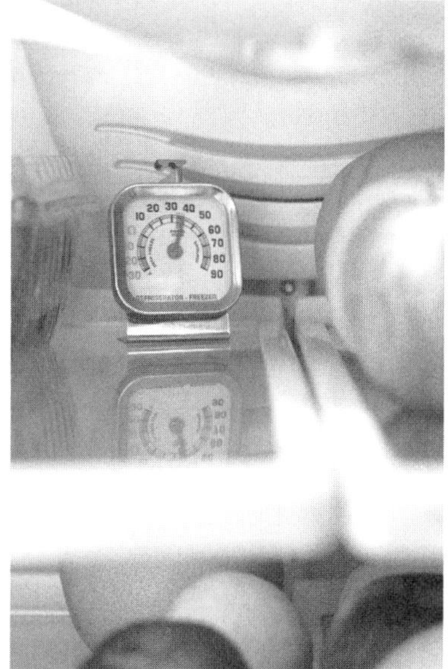

Shrinking the size of your refrigerator and freezer will also help perishables stay cold longer. Long before an anticipated storm, fill empty soda bottles with water. Be sure to leave an inch or more at the top as water expands as it freezes. Then place the bottles in the empty spaces in your refrigerator and freezer. Once cooled or frozen, the bottles will act as an insulator, helping to keep your perishables cold longer should the power go out.

When a blackout occurs, make note of the time so you'll have an idea of how long you can go before the food is unsafe to eat. The time will vary depending on whether the food was kept in the refrigerator or the freezer.

→ REFRIGERATOR

Food in the refrigerator should be safe as long as the door has been kept shut and the power is out less than four hours. If the power is out longer, or if the fridge door has been opened repeatedly, the food inside will need to be thrown away. Meat, chicken, fish, eggs, dairy products, lunchmeats, and last night's dinner leftovers need to be tossed if they have been stored above 40 degrees for 2 hours. Bacteria multiplies quickly at warm temperatures and eating the contaminated food will make you sick. Unfortunately, you can't tell if it's safe by the way it looks or smells and please never taste it to check its safety.

If it looks like you won't have electricity for more than four hours, start eating from your fridge before you pull from your pantry. As you get closer to the four-hour mark, you can move perishables from your refrigerator and pack them in coolers filled with ice to try to extend the shelf life. Then as you are about to cook or eat the items from the cooler, take their temperature with a food thermometer. If the temperature is 40° F or higher, don't risk your health. Just throw it away.

→ FREEZER

Food in the freezer will last up to 48 hours if the freezer is full and the door is kept closed. A half full freezer keeps food frozen for half that time—twenty-four hours. If the power comes back on during those time frames, the thawing food will still be safe to eat. As long as the freezer temperature never went above 40°F, or the food still contains ice crystals, it can be refrozen but the quality may not be to your liking.

If you anticipate the blackout will continue for more than two days, dry ice may be the solution for your freezer. If you decide to go this route, find a vendor now and when an blackout occurs, get there quickly. The vendor will be able to help you determine how much dry ice you need. If you purchase dry ice, use caution. With temperatures of -109° F, it's not something to fool with. Always follow the vendor's safety recommendations.

HOW TO KEEP WARM

After you lose electricity, your home will stay warm for a few hours as long as you limit the number of times you open exterior doors. Each time a door opens heat escapes and cold icy air comes in. Beyond that, there are a few strategies for staying warm, however if it looks like it will be a while before power's restored, make arrangements stay with a friend or consider going to a shelter or "warming center" before things get really bad.

→ ONE ROOM

First of all, forget trying to heat the whole house. A better strategy is to pick one room—preferably the smallest and definitely the one without the high ceiling. If you live in a two-story house, check to see if the upstairs is noticeably warmer. Rooms on the South side of the house will be warmer too because sun shining through the window heats the room as long as the blinds are open.

Once you've picked a room, make it your family hangout spot. Gather your family members and pets together. Grab couch cushions, blankets, and snacks. Shut the door and seal the room off with draft stoppers made from rolled towels. Place them on the windowsills and at the base of the closed door. When the sun goes down prevent heat from escaping the room by closing the blinds and covering the window with towels or blankets for insulation.

And now's not the time to be shy! Get as close as you can. Create a fort out of a blanket, have everyone pile in and let body heat do its thing. Surround yourselves with couch cushions and extra blankets. Think: bird's nest.

→ FIREPLACES

Do you have a fireplace? If you've kept up on the chimney cleaning and inspection, use it. If you've skimped on the maintenance, don't risk it. Soot and debris can easily catch fire and burn your house down. While fireplaces aren't great for keeping warm—most of the heat goes up the chimney—something is better than nothing. And if you don't have wood to burn, make logs out of tightly rolled newspaper and magazines.

Fireplaces outfitted with decorative gas logs may still be usuable in a blackout as long as gas lines weren't damaged. Depending on the model, your gas logs

may have a standing pilot that doesn't require electricity, or it may have a battery backup system that can be used to light the pilot. You might even be able to light the pilot manually with a long stem lighter. Consult your owner's manual to learn more about your model.

If you decide to use your fireplace, always be sure the flue is open and the room is well ventilated. And remember, barbeques are for outside. Never bring a grill—charcoal, gas or otherwise—in the house.

→ SPACE HEATERS

Fuel burning space heaters are dangerous and in many places illegal if not vented properly to the outside. Carbon monoxide poisoning, burns and house fires are the biggest risks with space heaters. More than 25,000 house fires and 300 deaths result from space heater use every year according to the U.S. Consumer Product Safety Commission. An additional 6,000 people end up in the emergency room for burn injuries after accidentally touching the hot surface of space heaters. If you decide to use a space heater, be sure your carbon monoxide detectors are working and follow the manufacturer's operating instructions and recommended safety precautions to the letter.

→ WARM CLOTHES

The best way to dress for the cold indoors is wear loose-fitting clothes and take the layered approach—a base, insulation and outer layer. The base layer is a thin, second skin-like layer that regulates your body temperature by controlling moisture. Think: thermal underwear, tights and t-shirts. Wool, silk, and synthetic fabric like polyester work best. Avoid cotton. Instead of wicking away moisture, cotton absorbs it, leaving you feeling cold and clammy.

The second layer, insulation keeps the warm air close to your body. Insulation layers are the layers you add or remove depending on how hot or cold you feel. Wool sweaters and fleece pullovers are common choices. The final layer called the outer layer acts as protection and keeps the elements away from your body. A thick winter jacket will fit the bill and then add your warm winter hat, scarf, gloves or mittens.

During winter power outages, hand and foot warmers are your best friends. My favorites, made by HotHands, provide up to ten hours of heat for your fingers and toes. Unfortunately, these air-activated heat packs can only be used once, so be sure to stock up.

HOW TO **KEEP KIDS ENTERTAINED** DURING A POWER OUTAGE

Kids think power outages are exciting for about 20 minutes then boredom sets in. Here are several things to do when you hear the dreaded phrase, "I'm bored."

- Play board games.
- Break out the deck of cards and play games like Go Fish, Memory, Old Maid, and War.
- Read a book.
- Tell stories.
- Do arts and crafts. Draw, color, make collages from old magazines or create sculptures out of aluminum foil.
- Have a pillow fight.
- Make an obstacle course. Roll across beds, crawl under tables and set up a jump rope or hula hoop station.
- Play flashlight hide and seek or flashlight tag.
- Go on a scavenger hunt.
- Have a playdate. It's always more fun to be bored with a friend.
- Step outside at night. Go star gazing or catch lightning bugs.
- Look at old photos.
- Sing!
- Play dress up. Accessorize with glowstick necklaces and bracelets.
- Go camping. Build a fort in the living room and tell ghost stories while eating raw s'mores.
- Get dramatic. Stage a play or put on a shadow puppet show.
- Pamper your girls. Brush and braid hair, then paint fingers and toes.
- Put together a puzzle.

HOW TO KEEP COOL

Power outages happen for a number of reasons, one of which is the extra demand air conditioners put on the power grid during a heat wave. Without air conditioners and electric fans, your home will heat up quickly. Here are some strategies for staying cool during a summer power outage.

➔ ONE ROOM

Your first instinct will be throw open the windows to get some air but this can actually make the situation worse. Once the air temperature outside is higher than inside, opening windows will actually make you hotter. Keep the windows closed while the sun is out. When it goes down, open the windows and doors and let the cooler air inside.

Just like you don't want to attempt to heat your whole house during a winter power outage, you don't want to try to cool it during a summer power failure. Do the opposite of everything you just learned about staying warm. Look for a North facing room in your house to serve as a cool retreat for your entire family as it usually has the least amount of sunlight coming through the windows. If you don't have a North facing room, rooms with windows that are blocked by trees, awnings or a neighbor's house are the second best choice. Also, the lowest level of your home will be cooler than the upper floors. Once you've located the best space, close the blinds and hang towels or sheets over the windows to keep the heat out. Make a solar reflector out of cardboard cut to the windows' size. Use aluminum foil to line one side of the cardboard. Keep the reflector, foil side out, in the windows to reflect the heat during the day.

Stone, tile and hardwood floors are cooler than carpet, hence the reason why your dog sleeps on the bathroom floor during the summer months. If you're still struggling to find relief from the heat, follow Fido's lead and lay down on the bare floor.

➔ WATER

Drink plenty of water to stay cool. Avoid caffeine and alcoholic beverages. They may raise your body temperature. Wet a bandana or t-shirt and wear it around your neck during the day. At night before bed, spritz water on your sheets with a spray bottle.

If you've ever been to Disney World in July, you would have seen crowds of people seeking heat relief in front of giant, water-misting fans. I know from experience that the misting fans work because my family hunted for Disney's fans more than we hunted for their princesses. The next time you make a trip to your local big box store, pick up a smaller, hand-held version of the Disney fan for everyone in the family. These little fans are battery powered so be sure you grab plenty of extra batteries.

→ COOL CLOTHES

Obviously, wearing your birthday suit during a heat wave works best but your family will probably think a bathing suit is a better idea. Not fond of bathing suits? Then wear a light, loose fitting outfit instead. Preferably one made of natural fabrics like cotton, linen or silk.

NO WORKING BATHROOM?

City water users, as long as your utility company's backup generators function, there will be water flowing from your tap, although it may not be safe to drink. And if your hot water heater is electric, expect the water to be cold. Any water you use for personal hygiene will have to be heated first using one of the powerless cooking options.

If you have a well, chances are your pump is electric so you won't have water. Using the bathroom becomes a problem. A toilet doesn't require electricity but the pump that refills it does. Manually pour water into your toilet to flush it. Your toilet may require a few gallons of water per flush so as gross as it sounds, don't flush after every use. If possible, don't use your drinking water supply for flushing. Use water from your swimming pool, a natural water source or recycled water—water collected before it goes down the drain—to get the job done.

MEDICAL EQUIPMENT AND MEDICATION CONSIDERATIONS

If someone in your house is dependent on refrigerated medication or electrical life-support devices, a power outage quickly changes from a minor annoyance to a life-threatening emergency. How do you keep medicine cool and equipment running?

→ MEDICATION

If the power is out for a few hours only, medicine will be fine in the refrigerator as long as the door remains shut and the fridge temperature stays at 40°F. If the blackout continues longer than three or four hours, it's possible the medicine will still usable. For example, according to the U.S. Food and Drug Administration, unaltered, undiluted insulin products in manufacturer's vials or cartridges maintain their effectiveness for up to 28 days as long as they are kept at a temperature between 59 and 86°F.

Never use ice to keep your medication cool. Insulin and other medications will lose their effectiveness if they freeze. Consider a FRIO Cooling Case (FRIOCase.com) instead. The liner in this reusable, wallet-like case is made of crystals, which expand into a cooling gel when it's soaked in water for five to ten minutes. Once activated, the FRIO case will keep medicine at or below room temperature in 100° weather conditions for up to two days before you need to re-soak it.

Be clear about the safety precautions your prescribed medication requires. Always consult with your pharmacist or physician.

→ MEDICAL EQUIPMENT

For power dependent medical equipment, you need to plan for an emergency backup ahead of time. Should you stock an extra battery or invest in a generator? Develop a power outage plan with the help of your doctor. Then, contact your power company and let them know you rely on life-saving medical equipment. Many utility companies offer programs for customers with special needs and are able to alert you prior to scheduled power outages. And some, but not all, will put you on a priority list for restoring electric service in the event of an emergency.

Portable Generators

Portable generators are popular among homeowners looking for emergency power. Simply set up the generator in your yard and run extension cords to your appliances. As long as you have a supply of gasoline to keep it fueled, you'll have backup electricity for your lights, refrigerator and medical equipment. Portable generators are valuable tools but there are a few things you need to know before you purchase one.

HOW TO CHOOSE A GENERATOR

Generators come in various sizes, or generator output which is measured in watts. Before you go shopping you should decide how many watts you need. Don't skip this important step because trying to draw more watts than a generator can produce will damage both the generator and the connected appliances.

Once you've decided on which appliances you absolutely can't live without in an emergency, write down the running wattage and starting wattage for each. Find this information in the owner's manuals or get estimates from an online generator wattage calculator, like the one found at briggsandstratton.com.

Add up all appliances' running wattage to get the total running watts. Then find the appliance with the highest starting wattage number. Add that number to the total running watts and you get the total starting watts. Choose a generator that produces no less than the total running watts number and total starting watts number.

GENERATOR SAFETY TIPS

Improper use of a generator can be deadly. Never use a generator without reading the owner's manual first and always follow the manufacturer's recommendations for safety.

After Hurricane Sandy, at least nine people died from carbon monoxide poisoning due to improper generator use. Never use a generator inside your house—and not in basements, garages, crawlspaces, sheds, porches, carports or any partially enclosed areas either. According to the US Fire Administration, one generator produces the same amount of carbon monoxide as hundreds of cars so don't think opening windows, doors or using fans will protect you from it's deadly effects. Set up your generator outside far away from doors and windows. A good rule of thumb is place it at least 15 feet away from your house as well as your neighbor's. And if you haven't done so already, install a carbon monoxide detector in your home.

Never plug a generator into a wall outlet. Portable generators are not intended to be connected directly to your home's wiring. Attempting to power your whole house through this dangerous process, known as back-feeding is extremely dangerous and often illegal. Power is not only sent back to your main breaker, it continues on to the transformer and energizes utility lines which can injure or kill workers who are attempting to restore the electricity to your neighborhood, even if they are working on lines that are miles away.

Using a generator during wet conditions poses a serious electrocution risk. Set it up on a dry surface and always be sure your hands are dry before touching it. If you must run the generator during rain or snow, use a tarp to create a canopy over it. When it's time to refuel, turn the generator off and let it cool for at least two minutes. If gasoline comes in contact with the hot engine or exhaust, it could ignite.

How to Store Fuel Safely

Gas, propane and charcoal may be hard to come by if a power outage lasts longer than a day or two. If you're thinking about keeping a fuel supply at home, learn how to store it safely.

GAS

Before you head to the pump, determine how much gas you'll need. The manufacturer's online specs for your generator should tell you the fuel tank capacity and the run time per tank. Then, check your local laws. Many communities prohibit homeowners from storing more than 25 gallons on their property and require gasoline to be stored in containers no larger than 5 gallons each.

The best containers for gasoline are approved red Underwriters Laboratory (UL) safety cans. The wording on the side will tell you if it meets safety requirements. Fill the containers 95% full to give gas room to expand if it warms up in storage. Cap the container tightly to prevent the gas from evaporating.

Never store gasoline in your house or attached garage. The ideal storage location is a well-ventilated area, away from your house. If you don't have a shed, make a storage locker or purchase a flammable liquid storage locker from a safety equipment supplier. Choose a location out of direct sunlight, away from children, electrical equipment, tools that might produce sparks and open flames. Don't store containers directly on concrete as it may degrade the plastic container. Just like you do for water storage, put down a layer of plywood or cardboard first.

Gasoline has a short shelf life. Properly stored in a clean container in the ideal location, it will only last a few months. For a longer shelf life, add a fuel stabilizer. Products, like Sta-Bil will keep gas fresh for up to 12 months. During that time, keep it in rotation. Use it for your lawn mower and put some in your car.

PROPANE

Gas grills belong outside and so do the propane tanks that fuel them. Never store spare tanks in your house, basement, garage or shed. Find an outdoor location, out of direct sunlight and away from your grill (no, you shouldn't store them underneath) and outdoor fire pits.

Store propane tanks upright in a place where they won't accidentally tip and roll around. And teach your kids not to play near them. Full or empty, be sure the cylinder valve on spare tanks remain closed, and capped or plugged.

Propane has an indefinite shelf life, however the tank itself has an expiration date of 12 years from manufacture date. You can find the expiration date stamped on the collar of the canister. By law, after 12 years the tank must go through a re-certification by a qualified propane retailer before it can be refilled. If you get your tanks from a grocery store tank exchange, always check the date before you drive off.

CHARCOAL

Charcoal absorbs moisture from the air so the best place to store it is in a cool, dry place. After a few months of sitting in an open bag in your garage it may be difficult to light. For an indefinite shelf life, put charcoal in an airtight, plastic or metal container. If you've purchased charcoal with lighter fluid already on the briquet, expect a shelf life of one to two years when stored properly in a container.

It's a Power Outage! Now What?

You've planned for it and now it's happening. Here are the steps you need to take as soon as the lights go out:

- Grab your flashlight.
- Turn off computers, printers, audio equipment, televisions and any appliances currently in use. Even with surge protectors, it doesn't hurt to be extra careful with sensitive electronics. In fact, I usually go one step further and unplug everything.
- Leave on one light so you'll know when the power is restored.
- Find out why the power went out. Check your fuse box then look to see if your neighbors have power. Still stumped? Call your power company and report the outage.
- If the power outage is disaster related, turn on your emergency radio and listen for information updates.
- Gather together the rest of your power outage supplies.

POWER OUTAGE KIT CHECKLIST

In addition to your family emergency kit, keep these power outage essentials in your home:

- ❑ Hand and foot warmers
- ❑ Sleeping bags
- ❑ Extra blankets
- ❑ Winter clothing
- ❑ Battery-powered, hand-held fans
- ❑ Spray bottle
- ❑ Candles
- ❑ Glowsticks
- ❑ Flashlights
- ❑ Headlamps
- ❑ Battery-powered or solar-powered lights
- ❑ Extra batteries
- ❑ Lighters and matches
- ❑ Powerless cooking stove of your choice
- ❑ Extra fuel
- ❑ Coolers
- ❑ Appliance thermometer
- ❑ Food thermometer
- ❑ Manual can opener
- ❑ Battery-powered emergency radio
- ❑ Battery-powered clock
- ❑ Battery-powered or solar-powered cell phone charger
- ❑ Cash in small denominations
- ❑ Power company's phone number plus your account number
- ❑ Five gallon bucket
- ❑ Construction grade trash bags with twist ties
- ❑ Antibacterial wipes and baby wipes
- ❑ Hand sanitizer
- ❑ Generator
- ❑ Extension cords
- ❑ Gas can
- ❑ Entertainment

CHAPTER 8

Be Ready to Stay or Go

When a disaster is bearing down on your home, you have two options. **You stay put or you go.** In this chapter, let's discuss what you need to know to be ready to stay at home or evacuate during an emergency.

Staying Put

Depending on the nature of the emergency you may need to stay at home anywhere from a few hours to a few days to a few weeks. Everything we've discussed so far—assembling an emergency kit, stocking your pantry, preparing for power outages and more—will come in handy if you need to stay sheltered in your home for any length of time. Also, as you determine what emergencies your family may face, ask yourself if you need to make additional plans for shelter. For example, if tornadoes are a threat to your area, choose a safe room in your house where your family can gather in the event a tornado occurs. And there's always the possibility you may be required to shelter-in-place.

Shelter-in-Place

When an emergency situation arises in your area, you may hear authorities say "Shelter-in-place." Shelter-in-place means it is too dangerous for you to be outside and the best way to stay safe is to find an indoor shelter immediately. Your indoor shelter might be your home, work, school, car or a public building. Basically, when you are told to shelter-in-place, you need to stay wherever you are.

Typically, authorities will advise you to shelter-in-place when there has been a man-made disaster of some kind that results in hazardous material in the air. It could be a due to a gas leak, an industrial fire, a chemical spill or a nuclear accident.

More often that not, shelter-in-place advisories are for the short term, lasting only a few hours rather than days or weeks. Once the wind has moved hazardous air or authorities have contained the situation you will be given the all clear.

Shelter-in-place advisories will come over the alert system. When you hear one, be sure to turn on your radio or television as they will be broadcasting the specific steps authorities want you to take. Then continue to listen so you will know when it is safe again.

HOW TO SHELTER-IN-PLACE

Your house is your first level of protection in a shelter-in-place scenario. However, in the event hazardous materials are in the air, you will want to seek extra protection in a safe room. Choose a room large enough for all the members of your family (including your pets!) and one that isn't too difficult to seal shut. The ideal safe room would have a bathroom attached and very few or no windows. Your basement may seem like a good choice but avoid setting up your safe room there. Some chemicals, like chlorine, are heavier than air and will seep in even if you closed and sealed the windows.

Next, take a trip to the local home improvement store. Purchase 2-4 mil plastic sheeting and duct tape. When you get home measure all the windows and doors. Add at least two inches all around and then cut the plastic sheeting to size. It will be easier to seal the windows and doors if the plastic is larger than the openings. Label each sheet because when you are in a panic, you won't want to be trying to figure out which sheet goes where. Store the plastic sheeting and duct tape in your safe room along with some blankets.

If you receive notice from the authorities to shelter-in-place, act quickly but don't panic. Whether you are at home, work or in the car, there are steps you can take to stay safe.

If you are at home, follow these steps:

- Seal your house by closing and locking all windows and exterior doors. If authorities warn you of potential explosions, close all the blinds and curtains.
- Close the fire place damper then turn off fans, plus your heating and air conditioning systems.
- Move your Go-Bags and emergency kit to the safe room.
- Direct your family to go to the safe room. Gather up your pets and don't forget to bring food and water for them.
- Tune into local news stations for emergency updates.
- Use duct tape to seal all windows and doors with the pre-cut plastic sheeting.
- Call or text members of your family who are away from home then get in touch with your out-of-area contact and let them know of your situation.
- Stay in the room until you are told it is safe to leave. It is possible the situation will get worse so be ready to evacuate if authorities tell you to do so.

If you are at work, you'll want to follow your workplace emergency plan. If a plan doesn't exist, take the same steps you would if you were at home. Enlist the help of co-workers to seal the building—closing and locking windows and doors, closing blinds and turning off air ventilation, air conditioning and heating systems. Assign a group to gather emergency supplies and select a safe room. Once everyone is in the room, stay tuned to the local news for information. Call your family and wait until authorities tell you it's safe to leave.

If you are in your car and you hear a shelter-in-place order come over the radio, keep driving if you're very close to your destination or a public building. Once you arrive, follow the same steps for shelter-in-place at home. Otherwise, take the following steps:

- Pull off the road and park. (In the summer, park in a shady place to keep from overheating.)
- Turn the heat or air off and close the vents. Close the windows then turn off the engine.
- Pull the duct tape out of your car emergency kit and tape over the vents.
- Turn on the radio every so often and listen for updated information on the situation.
- Stay parked until local officials tell you it's safe. When you do start driving again, be prepared for road closures and detours.

Whether you are at home, work or in your car, always follow your local emergency management officials' directions. They are on the front lines dealing with the situation so they are the best source of information.

SHELTER-IN-PLACE OR LOCKDOWN?

Recently, the phrase shelter-in-place has been used in place of the word lockdown. The term "lockdown" insinuates a threat of violence, usually in the form of an active shooter or another dangerous criminal. Authorities put out the shelter-in-place advisory to keep you inside for your own safety and also to keep you out of the way until they can apprehend the bad guy.

For example, during the search for the Boston Marathon bomber, the entire Boston area of more than a million people was asked to shelter-in-place for 12-plus hours. Public transportation was suspended, school was cancelled, offices were closed, and trains and buses were delayed.

When you hear "shelter-in-place" in this context, you will want to go indoors, however it isn't necessary to hole up in a sealed safe room. Just close, lock and stay away from all windows and external doors.

MANAGING EMOTIONS

Emergencies are stressful and so it's understandable if you are emotional when you are required to shelter-in-place. Your routine is disrupted, the situation is uncertain and you may even be separated from your loved ones. Knowing what emotions you may go through before the situation helps you to recognize the feelings later and cope with them.

You may feel anxious. With our busy lives, there is a real possibility that you won't be together when you receive the order to shelter-in-place. You or your spouse may be at work and your children may be at school. Unfortunately, the nature of the emergencies that require shelter-in-place are usually unexpected and keep you from getting to one another.

The uncertainty of the situation will probably weigh on your mind. Most likely you will have no idea how long you will be required to shelter-in-place. Will it be one hour or will it be 12?

And then there is fear. Emergencies that require you to shelter-in-place are frightening and it won't be uncommon for you to have concerns about your safety or your loved one's while you wait.

Most parents are pretty familiar with the emotion guilt. And if you are separated from your children, guilt is pretty much a given. You will feel guilty for not being there to help them through the situation. You may also feel guilty if sheltering-in-place keeps you from fulfilling your other responsibilities, like work.

Lastly, if you haven't taken the steps outlined in the previous chapters to ready your family with supplies, you will be distressed about your lack of resources, like food, water and medical supplies. If you have taken the steps but you are with people who haven't (co-workers) you may feel pressured to share your limited supplies.

Any one of these emotions is normal in an extremely abnormal situation. And remember, everyone handles stress differently. It's important to understand that whatever you are feeling may not be the same as what others are feeling.

So now that you know what emotions to expect, you need to have a plan for coping with them.

MAKE A **BUSY BOX**

An already stressful situation gets ten times worse when your little ones are complaining there's nothing to do. A busy box will keep your kids occupied in the car during an evacuation or in the safe room while sheltering-in-place. Grab an old shoebox or baby wipes container and fill it with things to entertain them. Here are some suggestions:

- Magnifying glass
- Slinky
- Magnetic letters in a metal lunch box
- Dry erase board with markers or a Magna Doodle
- Mad Libs
- Sticker books
- Post it Notes in assorted colors and sizes
- Colored pencils
- Paper
- Coloring books or activity books
- Glowsticks, glow necklaces or glow bracelets
- Pipe cleaners
- Balloons
- Small figurines or cars
- Band-Aids
- Lollipops
- Plastic Easter eggs filled with little treats
- Temporary tattoos
- MP3 player loaded with audio books
- Disposable camera
- Silly Putty
- Paper dolls
- Shoelaces and wooden beads
- Rainbow Loom

Once you've assembled the busy box, store it with your Go-Bags so it will always be handy when you need it.

- First, stay informed. Tune in to your emergency radio or television for the latest information from your local officials. While it will help to know what's going on around you, be careful not to become overexposed. You, and especially your children, may actually feel more stressed and afraid if you subject yourself to the media's repetitive news cycles.
- Also, remember to take care of yourself and your family. When my emotions are running high, I tend to skip meals and have a hard time sleeping. If you do too, make sure you get plenty to eat and drink and, depending on the hour, sleep. Encourage those around you to do the same.
- If you are separated from loved ones, get in contact. Talking to your children or spouse on the phone or by text and email will help relieve the stress. Don't forget to touch base with your out-of-area contact as well. Family members not involved in the emergency will be worried about you.
- Finally, be positive. Visualize a good outcome for everyone. If those around you are slipping in to negativity, help them to stay emotionally strong. If you are spiritual or religious, turn to the practices you find comforting in difficult times.

Evacuate

Sometimes it's just not safe to stay at home. Hurricanes, floods, wildfires and man-made disasters like industrial or nuclear accidents may force you to leave. Let's look at evacuation orders and how you can plan for them.

VOLUNTARY VERSUS MANDATORY EVACUATION

If your area is facing a threat, usually from a hurricane or wildfire, authorities may issue an evacuation warning. The purpose of an evacuation warning or voluntary evacuation is to alert you to danger and let you know that it's likely your life and property will be at risk in the future. Use this time to get your home prepared, fill up your gas tank, gather your supplies and make arrangements for some place to stay. Stay tuned in and listen for emergency updates and instructions.

When the order is voluntary, you may want to consider leaving so you can get out ahead of everyone else and avoid the inevitable traffic jam. But how do you know if you should leave? Would you be safe if you stayed? Evaluate your situation. How close is the danger? Will your home be a safe shelter? Does anyone in the

EMERGENCY **TOOL KIT**

Every home needs a good tool kit. These tools are useful for everyday home repairs and they will come in handy when you are preparing your home for a major event, such as a hurricane or wildfire. Here are some items to include:

- Duct tape
- Plastic sheeting
- Electrical Tape
- Claw Hammer
- Screwdriver set, flathead and phillips
- Work gloves
- Utility knife with extra blades
- Pliers; needle nose, groove joint, lineman's
- Wire cutter
- Socket wrench set
- Adjustable wrench set
- Pry bar
- Safety glasses
- Hatchet
- Hacksaw with extra blades
- Shovel
- Paracord
- Tarp
- Bungee cords
- Zip ties
- WD-40
- 5-gallon bucket
- Nails and screws in assorted sizes

family have special needs that will require extra time to evacuate? If you stay, will emergency services be available? Do you have all the supplies you need?

On the other hand, when your local officials order a mandatory evacuation, they are instructing you to leave your home immediately and head to a safer location. Mandatory evacuations are issued when injury or death to residents is likely or when the safety of first responders is in jeopardy. While no one is going to force you from your home, staying behind could be a violation of the law and result in a fine. Plus it's dangerous. When your area is under a mandatory evacuation, you can't count on emergency services to respond to your 9-1-1 call.

PLAN BEFORE AN EVACUATION

Start thinking about your evacuation plan before you need it. If you have ten minutes to evacuate your home, what would you take with you? Let's imagine for a minute how two families would react if a fireman knocked on their door and told them they had ten minutes to evacuate.

→ A TALE OF TWO FAMILIES

Family A has never thought about what they would do in a situation like this and they panic. For the first minute, Mom and Dad run confused circles around each other, wondering what to take. Mom directs the kids to go upstairs and get their toys and then she runs straight to the photo albums. Dad heads to the master bedroom to grab clothes and the cash he keeps in his top dresser drawer. From the kitchen, where she is packing juice boxes and snacks, Mom yells to Dad, "Did you get the kids' clothes?" The kids are also peppering Dad with questions. "Which doll should I take?" Ten minutes later everything is thrown haphazardly in the car. The kids are strapped in their car seats and the dog is in the way back. Just as they are about to pull out their driveway, Mom realizes she left her purse on the counter and makes a mad dash back inside. When she climbs back into the car, Dad looks at her and says "Where do we go?" They back out of the driveway not realizing that they left a change of clothes for Mom and the cell phone chargers behind.

Family B has a home evacuation plan. They've talked about what they would do and they've practiced it. Dad goes to the office to retrieve the Grab and Go Binder. Mom instructs the kids to go get Louie the sock monkey and the pink blanket then she opens the hall closet and pulls out the Go-Bags. When Dad returns from the office with the Grab and Go binder, he pulls out the Family Emergency Plan, the

Last Minute Checklist and the To-Do Chart. Mom glances at the chart and heads to the bathroom for the medication. Dad goes to the master bedroom and opens the safe. He stuffs cash and credit cards into his pocket. Next he goes through the house, making sure all the windows and doors are closed and locked. In the master bedroom, Mom grabs a change of clothes for her and Dad, along with her great-grandmother's wedding ring. Five minutes later they meet back at the front door with list in hand checking off the items. "Did you get the cell phones? How about the kids' winter jackets?" Eight minutes later, everything they need including the emergency kit is organized and in the car. The kids are strapped in their car seats and the dog is in the way back. As they pull out of the driveway and head to their friend's place, Mom dials the phone number of their out-of-area contact.

Now, who would you rather be? Thirty minutes of planning today can eliminate confusion and lessen panic.

→ MAKE A LAST MINUTE CHECKLIST

Sit down with your family and make a list of everything you will need to take with you when you leave. Obviously your Go-Bags should be first on the list since you assembled them specifically for an evacuation. And if that is all time will allow you to take, you will be able to sustain yourself for a few days. If you have more time, grab the rest of your emergency kit and any cash you have stashed around your house. If someone in your family is on medication or if they require medical equipment like a nebulizer, make sure you bring that too. Be sure you have clothes that are appropriate for the season and throw in a pair of sturdy shoes. Lastly, if there is room in your car, bring sentimental items that can't be replaced like photo albums and family heirlooms. When your list is complete, store it with your Family Emergency Plan.

→ ASSIGN RESPONSIBILITIES

After you created your Last Minute Checklist, talk about the action steps your family will need to take when you are told to evacuate. Write the steps down on a To-Do chart and divide the responsibilities among your family members. Who will grab the Go-Bags? Who will gather the pets? Who will turn off the utilities if the authorities instruct you to do so? During an emergency, our brains turn to mush. Relying on memory isn't the best plan. Your evacuation will go much smoother if everyone had written steps to follow. Once you have completed the To-Do chart, store it with your Family Emergency Plan.

I recommend you make a copy of the chart for each member of your family so everyone has their own list of responsibilities.

DECIDE WHERE YOU WILL GO

If you have to evacuate, obviously, you will need a place to go. The time to figure that out is before, not during, a crisis situation. For most of us, there are three options:

→ FRIENDS AND FAMILY

Is there a friend or family member outside of your area who is willing to host you in the event of an emergency? If yes, talk to them about your family's evacuation plan now instead of on the way to their house during a crisis.

→ HOTELS

Make a list of hotels and motels to the North, South, East and West of you along with their phone numbers. Keep the list handy in your Grab and Go Binder. If you know a hotel is your only destination option, don't wait until the evacuation begins to make reservations. Hotel and motel rooms fill up quickly and it will be difficult to find a vacancy—especially in the areas surrounding major cities.

→ SHELTERS

No one wants to stay in a shelter but if it's not safe to stay at home and you don't have the friends and family or hotel option, you may have no other choice. When you are making your emergency plan, inquire at your local emergency management office about shelter locations. Even if you were able to get an address to include in your plan, it's always best to listen for updates during the crisis as things may change. The locations of open shelters will be announced during emergency updates and the American Red Cross lists the shelters they manage on their website at http://www.redcross.org/find-help/shelter.

• WHAT TO BRING

Some shelters serve meals and some offer comfort kits filled with toiletries but beyond that, most don't provide much more than a cot and a roof over your head. Be sure to bring your family emergency kit along with your Go-Bags. Remember, this kit was made for situations like this. It will have food, water, medications and other daily necessities to keep you going for at least three days. If you haven't finished assembling your emergency kit yet (What are you waiting for?) you will need to show up at the shelter with these items for all members of your family:

- Food for minimum of three days
- Water, 1 gallon per person, per day
- Snacks
- Special diet foods for family members with dietary restrictions
- Prescription and over-the-counter medicine
- Eyeglasses or contacts
- Extra clothing (at least two complete outfits)
- Blanket or sleeping bag
- Pillows
- Entertainment—books, board games and deck of cards
- Beach or camp chair
- Identification
- Copies of insurance papers and other important documents
- Toiletries
- Infant needs—diapers, wipes, formula
- Elderly or special needs—hearing aids, dentures
- Flashlight with extra batteries
- Emergency radio with extra batteries
- Cell phone and charger
- First aid kit
- Medical supplies and equipment for family member with special needs along with a back-up power source
- Shelters do not take kindly to weapons, alcohol or illegal drugs, so it's best to leave those items home.

PLAN YOUR EVACUATION ROUTE

The first step in planning is to ask local officials about designated evacuation routes. Often there are signs marking the routes or you can find maps on the local emergency management department's website. Officials publicize the designated routes so you can become familiar with them ahead of an evacuation, however these routes may change in a crisis if they fall in the danger zone or are impassable due to the disaster.

Once you learn the designated evacuation routes, get a local map and identify two or more ways out of town in all directions. Mandatory evacuations have been known to cause colossal traffic jams. You need a plan B (and C and D!). Wouldn't you rather be high tailing it out of town on back roads instead of sitting in gridlock on the expressways?

Once you've mapped out your alternative routes, grab your map and GPS and drive them. If there are any holes in your plan, you will want to find them now, not in the middle of a mass exodus.

PETS

If you are told to evacuate for any reason, always, always take your pets with you! One reason there are so many homeless pets after a disaster is people think Fido and Fluffy will be more comfortable at home. They figure if they leave food out their pets (cats especially) will be fine until they get back. Or they misjudge the amount of time they will be away.

Back in chapter one, I recommended you develop an emergency plan for your pets. In your Grab and Go Binder you should have a list of vet hospitals, boarding facilities and pet-friendly hotels outside of your local area that might be able to assist you if you are forced to evacuate. When it looks like there is a possibility of a evacuation, get on the phone immediately and try to secure pet-friendly accommodations.

Another step in your planning was to contact your local emergency management officials and ask about shelters for pets. Prior to 2006, you weren't allowed to bring your pets to an agency run shelter and if you were evacuating on a bus provided by your local government, they made you leave your pets behind. Thankfully as a result of Hurricane Katrina, a law was passed requiring officials to make provisions for pets. Now, most communities will have a plan for sheltering

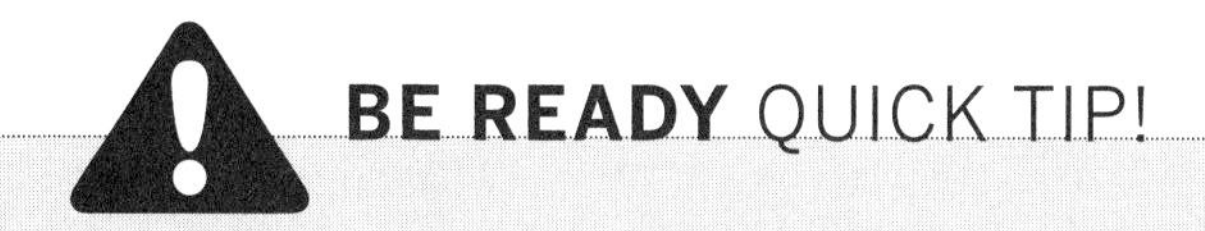

Hold an evacuation drill. Set a timer for ten minutes and go! Gather your items, then pack them in the car. Get together afterward to talk about what went right and what needs to be improved. Make changes to your plan if necessary.

your pets. Unfortunately, it doesn't necessarily mean your pets will be by your side. For example, in my community, trailers are set up to act as mini-boarding facilities, housing animals outside of the shelter. In other places, fairgrounds and racetracks are used to accommodate animals, both large and small. So, be sure to call authorities ahead of a disaster and ask, "Will there be shelters and services that accommodate pets in a crisis and what will they be like?"

Even if you find out your community has plans for pet-friendly shelters and services, you may not be able to rely on them in a large-scale disaster - they may be overwhelmed by the number of pets coming in. And frankly, they will have so much going on just dealing with people, your animals may not be a priority. Also some shelters (private ones run by churches and the Red Cross) still don't have to accept pets. Always have a few different evacuation plans up your sleeve and only go to a shelter if you absolutely have no other choice.

Finally, you will want to get your furry friend back if somehow you get separated. When my pups are home they don't wear their collars, so one of the responsibilities on our To-Do Chart is put the collars on the dogs. Make sure your animals are wearing identification when you evacuate.

It's Time to Evacuate! Now What?

The weather reports are predicting a major storm headed your way and officials have issued a voluntary evacuation order. What do you do?

First, decide when will you evacuate. Remember, once the evacuation is mandatory everyone will be hitting the road at the same time. It's pretty much guaranteed you'll be stuck in traffic. Stay tuned to the emergency updates and if conditions are deteriorating, hit the road early.

When leaving is your only option, refer to your plan. Pull out your Grab and Go Binder and find your Family Emergency Plan. Use your Last Minute Checklist and To-Do Chart. Instruct everyone to complete their tasks and meet at the car. Be sure to turn off utilities at the main shut off valves if the situation requires it. And don't forget to leave a note on your refrigerator stating when you left, where you are going and a phone number to contact you. Once you are on the road, call or text your out-of-area contact and let them know of your plans.

LAST MINUTE CHECKLIST

Below is a list of items you will need to take with you in an evacuation. Review the list and add other items that are specific to your family's needs Keep this list with your Family Emergency Plan.

- ❑ Go Bags
- ❑ Emergency kit (extra stash)
- ❑ Extra food
- ❑ Extra water
- ❑ Grab and Go Binder
- ❑ Computer or flash drives
- ❑ Cash
- ❑ Medication
- ❑ Medical equipment
- ❑ Self-defense item
- ❑ Jackets
- ❑ Sturdy shoes
- ❑ Blankets or sleeping bags
- ❑ Pillows
- ❑ Comfort items for kids

- ______________________________
- ______________________________
- ______________________________
- ______________________________
- ______________________________
- ______________________________

TO-DO CHART

List everything that needs to be done prior to leaving home.
Assign each family member a task to ensure a smooth evacuation.

TASK	NAME:	NAME:	NAME:	NAME:
Get the Grab and Go Binder (contains the Family Emergency Plan)				
Get the emergency kit, including Go-Bags				
Turn off utilities if necessary				
Gather pets and pet emergency kit				
Load supplies in the car				
Leave an evacuation note on the refrigerator				
Close and lock all windows and exterior doors				
Call out-of-area contact				
Listen to the radio for instructions from local officials				

UNPREPARED

CHAPTER 9

Be Ready for a Natural Disaster

Nature is unpredictable and no one is immune from her wrath. Every year, natural events like tornadoes, hurricanes, earthquakes, wildfires, floods, severe thunderstorms and winter storms are responsible for loss of life and property. Once you find out what natural disaster could affect your area, learn what to do **before, during and after** the event. This knowledge is an essential part of your family emergency plan.

Tornadoes

No matter where you live there is always the chance you could be caught in a tornado. Called nature's most violent storm, tornadoes are capable of producing winds of up to 300 miles per hour and destructive paths one-mile wide by 50-miles long. The storm's fury is unmatchable. In a matter of seconds a tornado can destroy large buildings, lift 20-ton railroad cars off their tracks and level an entire community. Make a plan now to be ready for a tornado.

WHAT TO DO BEFORE A TORNADO

- Review your family-emergency plan and make sure your emergency kit is fully stocked.
- Find out if your homeowner's insurance policy covers tornado damage.
- Regularly trim trees, removing the dead limbs to reduce the flying debris during a tornado.
- Be sure your children have memorized what county or area you live in and know how to listen for it on radio or TV updates.
- Designate a safe room in your house where everyone, including pets, should gather during a tornado. Some options are a storm cellar, basement or a window-less interior room, like a hallway, bathroom or closet on the lowest level of your house.
- If you live in a mobile or manufactured home, find the location of the nearest storm shelter and make a plan to get there quickly.
- Review the emergency procedures for the places your family frequents such as school or work, and identify safe shelters at each location.
- Know what alert systems sound like, including tornado sirens. Check with your wireless provider to see if your cell phone and service area is set up to receive Wireless Emergency Alerts (WEA) warning of dangerous weather in your area.
- Practice tornado drills. Go to the safe room and practice "duck and cover," crouching on the ground and protecting your head with your arms. Even better, have everyone in your family fitted for a bike or construction helmet and store them near or in your safe room.
- When stormy weather is forecasted, secure all loose items in the yard, like lawn furniture and trash cans to prevent them from becoming flying missiles.
- During a storm, keep an emergency radio with extra batteries handy and listen to local news for information on tornado warning and watches.
- Keep your eyes on the sky and look for signs of a tornado: a dark, often greenish color sky, hail or heavy rain, a large dark, low lying cloud, whirling dust or debris on the ground, a funnel cloud, or a loud roar that sounds like never ending thunder or a freight train.

WHAT TO DO DURING A TORNADO

- If you're in a house or building, grab a sturdy pair of shoes and your battery-powered radio, go to your designated safe room and "duck and cover". If possible get under a sturdy table, climb into a bathtub or put a mattress over you.
- Stay away from all windows and do not open them.
- If you are in a mobile or manufactured home, leave as soon as you receive a tornado warning and go to your designated shelter.
- If you are in a car, make sure your seat belt is buckled. Attempt to drive to the nearest shelter. If flying debris starts to hit your car, pull off the road and park. Turn off the engine. Keep your seat belt fastened and "duck and cover", making sure your head is lower than the windows. Or get out of your car and get lower than the road by lying in a ditch and covering your head with your arms.
- Tornadoes are fast and unpredictable. Never try to outrun a tornado with your car. Also, never take shelter under a highway overpass or bridge. These become a dangerous wind tunnel during a tornado.

WHAT TO DO AFTER A TORNADO

- Keep listening to your battery powered emergency radio for information and warnings of possible subsequent tornadoes.
- Check everyone for injuries and apply first aid if needed. Don't move anyone with serious injuries unless they are in danger.
- Do whatever you can to attract attention to your location if you are trapped.
- Don't go outside until you are absolutely sure the storm is over.
- Keep your shoes on at all times and watch where you step. Studies have shown that almost 30% of post-tornado injuries are from stepping on nails.
- Use extreme caution when exiting or entering a your home. Beware of downed power lines or objects that are touching downed power lines. Report any electrical hazards to the proper authorities.
- If your home has been damaged, turn off main utility valves to prevent explosions or electrocution.
- Keep your pets on leashes at all times to prevent them from becoming injured or lost.
- Implement the communications portion of your family emergency plan. Stay off the phone except to make an emergency call. Text message family members instead.

Hurricanes

If you live in a coastal area, there's a chance you could experience a hurricane. Houses along the coastline are most vulnerable but hurricanes can also cause damage several hundred miles inland. These large storms are capable of producing winds in excess of 155 miles per hour, heavy rainfall and storm surges—an abnormal and dangerous rise in sea level. Tornadoes, floods, and landslides can also occur as a result of a hurricane.

WHAT TO DO BEFORE A HURRICANE

- Review your family-emergency plan and make sure your emergency kit is fully stocked.
- Find out if your property is at risk for flooding. If yes, consider purchasing a flood insurance policy.
- Get familiar with the hurricane evacuation routes and make arrangements for a place to stay if you have to evacuate.
- Review your evacuation plan for pets and make any necessary changes.
- Know the difference between a hurricane watch and a hurricane warning. A hurricane watch means a storm with sustained winds 74 mph or higher is possible in your area within 48 hours. A hurricane warning is issued when a storm with sustained winds of 74 mph or higher is expected to hit your area within 36 hours.
- Do a quick clean up around your home. Clear rain gutters and downspouts. Trim trees and bushes. Bring in or secure all loose items in the yard, like lawn furniture and trash cans.
- Protect your home's doors and windows with permanent storm shutters or plywood cut to fit your doors and windows. Then strengthen your garage doors with braces if you don't have a wind-resistant model.
- Fill up the gas tank in your car and buy fuel for generators and grills.
- Test and prepare your generator.
- Fill empty soda bottles with water and place them in your refrigerator and freezer. Then turn refrigerator and freezer to their coldest settings.
- Clean the bathtub and fill it with water. Fill as many large containers as you can with water also.
- Get your power outage supplies ready.
- Move your car into the garage or park it near your home away from trees and utility poles.

WHAT TO DO DURING A HURRICANE

- Keep an emergency radio with extra batteries handy and listen to local news for weather information and evacuation orders.
- Move your Go-Bags near the door and gather your pets in one room in case you need to evacuate.
- Turn off utilities at the main shut off valves only if told to do so by authorities.
- Stay inside and stay away from windows and doors. It's a good idea to gather the family and pets together and go to safe room—a first level room in the center of your home.
- Stay off the phone except for emergencies.
- Be aware that a lull in the storm is often the "eye" of the storm and that the winds may pick up again.
- If you are told to evacuate, leave right away! Don't wait until the last minute. Plan on travel time to take at least twice as long. Also, notify your out-of-area emergency contact that you are evacuating.

WHAT TO DO AFTER A HURRICANE

- Keep listening to your emergency radio for weather updates and information.
- Flooding is possible even after the storm is over, so stay alert.
- If you stayed home during the storm, don't drive unless it's absolutely necessary. If you do venture out, don't drive on flooded roads and watch for downed power lines.
- If you evacuated, don't return home until authorities say it's safe.
- Check your home for damage. Stay out of your home if there are flood waters, structural damage, gas leaks or you have any doubts about it's safety. If necessary, have a qualified building inspector come out and give you the all clear before you enter.
- Report dangling or downed power lines to your utility company.
- Don't use tap water until authorities say it's safe to drink.
- Keep your pets on leashes at all times to prevent them from becoming injured or lost.
- Practice generator safety.
- Let your out-of-area emergency contact know your family is safe then stay off the phone.

Earthquakes

An earthquake is sudden trembling or shaking of the earth's surface, a result of a sudden release of pent up energy between two moving blocks of earth called plates. If severe enough, an earthquake can flatten an entire city. You may think you are free and clear of the earthquake risk but think again. Earthquakes can happen in any of the fifty states. And since scientists haven't figured out a way to predict when and where an earthquake will take place, it's important that your family be ready for one.

WHAT TO DO BEFORE AN EARTHQUAKE

- Review your family-emergency plan and make sure your emergency kit is fully stocked.
- Identify a safe spot in each room of your house, such as under a solid piece of furniture or in the corner of an interior room. Don't forget to locate a safe spot at the places you frequent like work or school.
- Conduct earthquake drills with your family. Practice the internationally recognized earthquake safety strategy, "Drop, Cover and Hold On". Drop to the floor and move to the room's safe spot. Take cover under a table. (If a table isn't available, crawl to the inside corner of the room and cover your head with your arms.) Hold on until the shaking stops.
- Bolt anything that could fall—bookshelves, china cabinets, tall furniture, and big-screen TVs—to the wall studs. Secure overhead light fixtures and strap water heaters, furnaces, gas appliances and refrigerators to the wall.
- Don't hang heavy pictures and mirrors near beds and couches.
- Keep a flashlight with spare batteries and shoes next to your bed in case an earthquake occurs in the middle of the night.
- Don't set your bed in front of a window. And make a habit of closing the bedroom window blinds at night. This will prevent breaking glass from flying into the room during a nighttime earthquake.
- Ask your gas utility company if they recommend an automatic gas shut-off valve for your home.
- Don't put off home repairs. If your house has structural problems like a cracked

foundation or ceilings, it has little chance of holding up against an earthquake.

- Store heavy and flammable items on lower shelves, closest to the ground.
- Keep breakable items like glass and china safe in a cabinet with doors that latch shut.

WHAT TO DO DURING AN EARTHQUAKE

- Drop, cover and hold on! If an earthquake happens while you're in bed, stay there. Cover your head with pillows and hold on until the shaking stops.
- Never flee from your house or building. Stay inside until you are sure the shaking has stopped.
- Never use an elevator.
- If you're outside during an earthquake, stay outside and drop to the ground. Don't try to run into a building for cover and keep away from power lines, trees, signs and street lights.
- If you are driving, pull over and stop. Don't park under overpasses or on bridges. Stay in your car with your seat belt on. When the shaking stops, drive carefully. Watch out for road damage and downed power lines.

WHAT TO DO AFTER AN EARTHQUAKE

- Expect aftershocks. They may not be as strong as the main earthquake but they still can cause damage or injury. If one occurs, drop, cover and hold on.
- Check everyone, including yourself, for injuries. Apply first aid if necessary.
- Turn on an emergency radio and listen for information from local officials. If you live on the coastline, be alert to the possibility of a tsunami. Listen for tsunami warnings.
- Shut off main utility valves if necessary. Check your home for structural damage or seek help from a qualified building inspector.
- Report downed power lines to the power company.
- Clean up any hazardous chemical or flammable liquid spills.
- Use caution as you open cabinet doors and closets. Objects will have shifted and something could fall on you.
- Implement the communications portion of your family emergency plan and let your out-of-area contact know your family is safe. Then stay off the phone.
- Keep your pets on leashes at all times to prevent them from becoming injured or lost.
- If you are trapped, never light a match. If there is a gas leak, the flame will cause an explosion. Signal for help by tapping on a pipe or on the wall. Avoid screaming because you may inhale toxic dust.

Wildfires

In 2013, 4.3 million acres were lost to wildfires. According to the National Association of Foresters, more than 72,000 communities in the United States face the risk of wildfires as more and more of us are building homes in or near woodland areas. Every family needs to be ready for a house fire but if your family is at risk for wildfires, you'll want to take a few more precautions.

WHAT TO DO BEFORE A WILDFIRE

- Review your family-emergency plan and make sure your emergency kit is fully stocked.
- Use fire resistant building materials for your home improvement projects.
- Choose fire resistant trees and shrubs when landscaping. For example, pines, evergreens and fir trees are more flammable than hardwoods.
- Hang wire mesh screen under porches, patios and decks to prevent leaf debris from accumulating under your home. Also, screen your attic vents and eaves.
- Inspect your roof. If there are loose or missing shingles, make the necessary repairs, as they are the best defense against embers getting inside your home.

BE READY TO MAKE AN INSURANCE CLAIM

The following tips can help the claims process go smoothly:

- Call your insurance company ASAP! Describe in detail the damage to your home and give two phone numbers where you can be reached.
- To help move the claims process along, take lots of photos or a video to document the damage before you start to clean.
- Make temporary repairs, like boarding up broken windows and covering holes in the roof. Any more than that and the insurance company may deny a claim because they can't determine what was done during the disaster or after.
- Keep invoices and receipts for cleanup and temporary repair expenses.
- Don't make permanent repairs until the adjuster has been out to your home.
- Most importantly, keep a record of all conversations, correspondences and estimates.

- Maintain a 30-foot buffer zone around your house. Trim trees, rake leaves, and mow grass. Also remove leaf piles, trash and woodpiles. Keep your grill away from your home. Water your lawn and landscaping and keep your gutters clear of leaf debris.
- Purchase household tools that can double as fire fighting tools—an axe, shovel, rake, bucket, saw, garden hose plus a ladder that can reach your roof.
- Know two routes out of your neighborhood.

WHAT TO DO DURING A WILDFIRE

- Listen to your emergency radio for information including health warnings about smoke.
- Make arrangements to stay with an out-of-area friend or family member in case you need to leave.
- If you go outside, dress for protection. Wear sturdy shoes, long pants, long-sleeved shirt, work gloves and a bandana over your nose and mouth.
- Gather your pets together in one room. If you need to leave in a hurry, you'll know where to find them.
- Put your emergency kit, including your Grab-and-Go Binder in the car. Then back the car into the garage or park it facing the street for a quick getaway.
- Set up lawn sprinklers on the roof and keep them running as long as possible.
- Get your fire fighting tools together.
- If you have a pool or hot tub, fill it with water. Also fill trash cans and any other large containers. Then keep the garden hose connected to the water spigot.
- Shut all windows, doors, vents and blinds to prevent smoke from getting inside. Turn off your air conditioning.
- Close the interior doors in your house. Then open the fireplace damper before you close the fireplace screens or doors.
- Turn off the natural gas and electricity at the main shut off valves.
- Move your furniture to the center of your home, away from windows and doors. Also bring flammable patio furniture inside.
- Make your house visible through smoke. Turn on the outside lights and leave at least one light on in every room.
- If authorities tell you to evacuate, leave immediately. Tell someone that you're leaving and where you are going.
- If you see the wildfire but haven't been told to evacuate, call 911 and report it.

7 WAYS TO HELP YOUR **KIDS COPE** AFTER A NATURAL DISASTER

A large scale natural disaster is a scary event for everyone and it can be especially traumatic for kids. Here are seven things you can do to help your children through the experience:

1. Hug them. Your physical touch is reassuring and so is your presence. You will have a lot on your plate after a disaster but set aside some time to spend with your little ones—even if it's just ten minutes before bed.

2. Give them a chance to talk. Encourage your kids to talk about their feelings. Answer any questions they have about what happened and find out what they're worried about. Don't be surprised if they ask the same questions over and over. Repetition is their coping mechanism. Always acknowledge their fears but also reassure them. Let them know their feelings are normal and most importantly, let them know they are safe.

3. Get back to a routine as soon as possible. Kids feel confident and safe when they have a routine. Unfortunately, there's no way around it—disasters disrupt routines. Try to maintain a normal meal and bedtime schedule. And until you can get back into the swing of things let your little ones know any disruption is only temporary.

4. Take care of yourself. Research has shown that a child's stress level after a natural disaster is directly impacted by his parents' stress. Children rely on the adults in their life to take care of problems and if they see you're struggling they will feel insecure. Take steps to alleviate your stress. Accept help when it's offered. Talk about your fears and concerns with another adult, instead of your kids. Get plenty to eat and be sure to rest.

5. Assign a job. It's not unusual for children to feel helpless after a disaster. Give them an age appropriate task and they'll feel like they are contributing to the recovery effort.

6. Turn off the television. Watching images of the disaster played over and over on the news will only cause more anxiety.

7. Seek professional help. After a disaster you should expect to see some changes in your children's behavior, such as clinginess, bed-wetting, irritability, depression or a lack of concentration. But if the behavior changes or isn't getting better over time, talk to your pediatrician about counseling.

WHAT TO DO AFTER A WILDFIRE

- Apply burn first aid if necessary. Call 911 for severe burns.
- If you evacuated, stay away until authorities say it's safe to return.
- Protect your hands and feet from hidden embers and hotspots. Wear leather work gloves and sturdy shoes.
- Watch out for ash pits. These dangerous holes full of hot ashes are the result of burned trees and stumps. If you find one, mark it for safety and warn others. Falling into an ash pit can cause severe burns.
- Check the roof and attic. Extinguish any fires, embers or sparks. Recheck several times over the next few hours.
- Use caution around burned trees and power poles, as they may not be stable.
- Beware of downed power lines and report any to the utility company.
- Do not turn on your home's utilities without a qualified technician's help.
- Wet ash and debris to reduce the amount of dust particles in the air.
- Follow the local public health department's guidelines regarding fire ash cleanup.
- Throw away food and medication that was exposed to heat and smoke as well as cleaning products, paint, batteries, and damaged fuel containers.
- Do not open your fire resistant safe right away. Intense heat stays trapped inside for several hours. Opening it before it has cooled completely can cause your valuables to ignite.
- Keep your pets on leashes at all times to prevent them from becoming injured or lost.
- Implement the communications portion of your family emergency plan and let your out-of-area contact know your family is safe.

Floods

Floods are the most common natural disaster and they can happen anywhere. Contrary to popular belief, you don't have to live near water. As long as there is rain or snow, there's a chance of flood. And because floods usually come with little or no warning, you will want to have a plan in place.

WHAT TO DO BEFORE A FLOOD

- Review your family-emergency plan and make sure your emergency kit is fully stocked.
- Find out if your home is at risk. Contact your local government and ask to see flood

zone maps. Or visit floodsmart.gov and view the Federal Emergency Management Agency's Flood Hazard Maps.
- Consider purchasing a flood insurance policy.
- Know two evacuation routes out of your neighborhood and out of the area.
- If your home is at risk, elevate your furnace, water heater and electrical panel. Install backflow valves in sewer lines to prevent floodwater from backing up into your home.

- Consider more elaborate protection measures. Construct berms and flood walls or add drains. Waterproof your basement walls with a sealing compound that prevents seepage.

WHAT TO DO DURING A FLOOD

- Listen to your emergency radio for flood warnings and reports about flooding in progress.
- Move your Go-Bags near the door in case you need to evacuate.
- Gather your pets together in one room. If you need to leave in a hurry, you'll know where to find them.
- Don't let your children play in the water.
- If authorities tell you to evacuate, leave immediately for higher ground. Tell someone that you're leaving and where you are going.
- If you have time, bring in outdoor furniture, move your valuables to upper floors and turn off the utilities at the main shut off valves.
- Never walk through moving water. It only takes six inches of moving water to knock you off your feet. If you have to wade through floodwater, look for standing water and use a stick to check the firmness of the ground before you step.

BE READY QUICK TIP!

Watch out for wildlife—especially poisonous snakes—that may have taken up residence in your home after the disaster. Use a stick to tap on walls and poke through debris. If you find a critter, leave a window open to encourage the animal to leave on its own.

- Avoid driving on flooded roads. If you are caught in your car during a flood, as long as the water isn't moving or deep, get out and move to higher ground. If the water is moving, stay in your car unless it's filling the car. In that case, get out and climb on top of the roof.

WHAT TO DO AFTER A FLOOD

- Keep listening to your emergency radio for weather updates and information.
- If you evacuated, don't return home until authorities say it's safe.
- Stay out of floodwater as it can be contaminated by gasoline, oil or sewage.
- Never step in standing water or puddles around downed power lines. Report them to the authorities or the power company.
- Wear rubber boots and rubber gloves to protect yourself from contaminants.
- Do not enter your house if it's surrounded by floodwater. Once the water has receded, use extreme caution upon entering, as it may be unstable.
- Throw away food, including canned food that came in contact with floodwater.
- Don't use tap water until authorities say it's safe to drink.
- Clean and disinfect all items that got wet.
- Implement the communications portion of your family emergency plan and let your out-of-area contact know your family is safe.

Severe Thunderstorms

Although they can happen year round, thunderstorms are more common in the spring and summer. Lightning is the biggest threat but severe thunderstorms can lead to tornadoes, floods and wildfires.

WHAT TO DO BEFORE A SEVERE THUNDERSTORM

- Review your family emergency plan and make sure your emergency kit is fully stocked.
- Download a weather app on your smartphone so you will receive alerts no matter where you are.
- Stay on top of tree trimming. Remove dead limbs or trees that could fall and cause injury during a storm.
- Talk to your kids about lightning safety and what to do during a severe thunderstorm.
- Keep your eye on the sky and reschedule outdoor activities if a storm is approaching.
- Unplug appliances and sensitive electrical equipment.

WHAT TO DO DURING A SEVERE THUNDERSTORM

- Get inside! And don't forget to bring your pets with you.
- Gather your family together in a safe room away from glass doors, windows and skylights.
- Listen to your emergency radio for weather updates.
- Stay away from the plumbing. Don't bathe, shower, wash dishes or do laundry during a thunderstorm.
- Stay off landline phones.
- Don't go out on the porch to watch the storm.
- Remain inside for thirty minutes after the last thunderclap.
- If you are caught outside with no shelter, seek low ground. Stay away from water, tall trees, sheds, picnic shelters and metal objects.
- If you are in your car during a severe thunderstorm, pull off the road and park. Turn on your hazard lights and don't touch any metal surfaces inside or outside the car.

WHAT TO DO AFTER A SEVERE THUNDERSTORM

- Keep listening to your emergency radio for updates.
- If you are driving, avoid flooded roads.
- Beware of downed power lines and report any to the utility company.

Winter Storms

Snow can be beautiful in the winter but when the weather reports are forecasting a winter storm, watch out! High winds, sleet, heavy snowfall, icy conditions and extreme cold can trap a family at home for days, sometimes without power.

WHAT TO DO BEFORE A WINTER STORM

- Review your family-emergency plan and make sure your emergency kit is fully stocked.
- Winterize your home. Insulate walls, attics and pipes. Apply weather stripping to windows and doors.
- Keep up with heating equipment maintenance. Schedule an inspection and cleaning once a year.
- Every winter, install storm windows or cover the interior side of your home's windows with plastic.
- Be sure you have snow shovels and a supply of rock salt and sand.

- Store extra heating fuel.
- Have warm clothing and extra blankets on hand.
- Know how to turn off the main water valve in case a pipe bursts.
- Be sure your car is stocked with emergency supplies.
- Stay current with your car maintenance. Regularly check your tires, brakes, fluid levels, cable connections, lights, windshield wipers and battery. Lubricate the door locks to keep them from freezing.
- Keep your gas tank near full to prevent the fuel lines from freezing.

WHAT TO DO DURING A WINTER STORM

- Stay home and stay inside. Don't drive unless it's an emergency. If you do venture out, don't travel alone. Also, tell someone where you are going and the route you will take.
- Keep an emergency radio with extra batteries handy and listen to local news for weather information.
- Bring your pets inside.
- Get your power outage supplies ready.
- To prevent pipes from freezing, open the cabinet doors under sinks so warm air can circulate around the plumbing. Also, let hot and cold water trickle from your faucets.
- If you are stranded in your car, pull off the road and turn your hazard lights on. Stay in the car. Don't go looking for shelter unless you can see a building close by. Run the heater for ten minutes every hour but take care to prevent carbon monoxide poisoning. Crack a window and keep snow out of the car's exhaust pipe.

WHAT TO DO AFTER A WINTER STORM

- When you are outside, wear proper winter clothing—warm, loose fitting layers plus a jacket, hat and gloves—to prevent frostbite and hypothermia.
- Be careful. Walkways will be slippery.
- If you have to shovel snow, take it slow. Don't overexert yourself.
- If power is out for an extended period of time, make arrangements to stay with a relative or friend who has heat.

SCHOOL'S CLOSED!
A NATURAL DISASTER FOR WORKING PARENTS

Kids love snow days. Parents? Not so much. To ease snow day stress, make a child care plan long before a school-closing catastrophe, a delayed start disaster or an early dismissal emergency strikes. Here are three things you can do:

1. Work it out with your spouse. Who stays home with the kids may depend on who has the most sick or vacation days. Or it may depend on whose job is the most flexible. If all things are equal, then take turns staying home or consider splitting the day in two shifts. You work in the morning and your spouse works in the afternoon.
2. Talk to your employer. What are the company's policies? Are you able to work from home? Does your employer allow flex hours or can you bring your kids to work? It doesn't hurt to ask and you may be surprised by what you learn. Some companies offer back-up care under their employee benefits plan. You may still have to pay for childcare but it can be less expensive than hiring a sitter on your own.
3. Start looking for your own back-up care. Do you have a family member nearby that you could rely on to help in a pinch? Would a stay-at-home mom agree to watch your children during the day in exchange for a night out? And don't forget, if your kids are out of school, the high schoolers are too. Is there a teenager that you could hire to baby-sit? Could you band together with other working parents and trade off childcare? You stay home and watch all the kids this time and next time, it's their turn. Lastly, investigate professional daycare options. Could you leave your school-aged children at your infant's day care provider or is there a drop-in childcare center near you?

CHAPTER 10

Be Ready for House Fires

According to the National Fire Prevention Association, you have a **one in four chance** of experiencing a house fire large enough to need to call for firefighters' assistance. Does that statistic surprise you? It sure surprised me. I didn't get serious about being ready for home fires until a house in my neighborhood burnt to the ground. When that happened, I realized a home fire really could happen to my family and it would be devastating. This chapter will focus on how you can prevent a home fire emergency as well as how to plan and practice for one.

Prevention

Whenever I read a news story about a house fire, I always look for mention of the cause. There are some unusual ones, like the house fire caused by the homeowner who attempted to exterminate a spider with a homemade blow torch. Yes, it's true. But for the most part, there are similarities. Let's take a look at the most common causes of house fires and how we can prevent them.

COOKING

Cooking is the number one cause of house fires and most cooking related fires happen because cooking food is left unattended. Don't get distracted in the kitchen. If you're frying, grilling or broiling food always stay by the pan. When oil gets too hot, it splatters. If you are not there to turn down the heat, it can ignite and start a pan fire. Simmering, baking, boiling or roasting? It's okay to step away for a minute but set a timer to remind you to return. Here are some more ways to prevent fires while cooking:

- Keep anything that can catch fire—paper towels, hand towels, oven mitts, wood utensils, oil, and curtains—a good distance away from the stove top while cooking.
- Always start with a clean stove top. Hot burners can easily ignite splattered grease spots and spilled food. Make it a habit to thoroughly clean the stove after every cooking session.
- Always keep the pan's lid or a cookie sheet near by in case of a pan fire.
- Watch your sleeves. Loose clothing can touch a burner and ignite. It's a good idea to wear short, close-fitting sleeves while cooking.

HOW TO PUT OUT A **PAN FIRE**

Never move a pan that's on fire. When you try to carry a burning pan to the sink the movement gives the fire air, making the fire worse. Also, never pour water onto a pan fire. Water mixed with the flaming oil causes a fire ball to erupt from the pot, spreading the fire in seconds. The best thing you can do is smother the fire. Cover the pan with a lid or cookie sheet and turn off the heat. Leave the lid on until the pan cools completely. Lifting it too soon allows air back in and can re-ignite the fire.

Q: IS IT SAFE TO LEAVE A **SLOW COOKER** ON WHEN I'M NOT HOME?

A: According to Crockpot, yes. Slow cookers are designed not to be fire hazards. While the outer heating base gets hot as it cooks, it will not set fire or cause your countertop to get too hot. That said, here are five steps you can take be extra fire safe:

- Use only an Underwriters Laboratories approved product. Look for the UL stamp on the base of the slow cooker or on its packaging.
- Always follow the manufacturer's safety recommendations outlined in the owner's manual.
- Never use your slow cooker with an extension cord.
- Clear the counter top around the slow cooker when in use.
- Make sure your slow cooker is the only thing plugged into the outlet.

- Wait for hot grease to cool before you throw it in a garbage can as it can cause trash to ignite.
- Before going to bed or leaving the home, check the kitchen. Are the stove, oven and small appliances turned off?
- Install StoveTop FireStops over your stove. These cans hang magnetically from your range hood. If flames touch the bottom of the can, it pops open and drops a chemical suppressant on the fire, putting it out. (www.stovetopfiresstop.com)

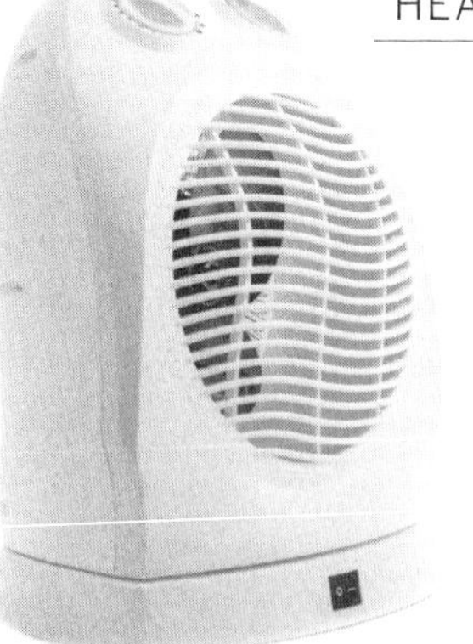

HEATING EQUIPMENT

Fourteen percent of all home fires are caused by heating equipment such as furnaces, fireplaces and space heaters. Space heaters are especially dangerous as they account for a third of heating-related fires and four out of five heating-related fire deaths. If you plan on using a space heater, remember, space heaters need space. Keep anything that could burn—blankets, papers, clothing, upholstered furniture—at least three feet away from a space heater. For the best chance of preventing heating-related fires, always...

- Use a space heater with an automatic shut off that activates if the unit tips over. Newer model space heaters are more likely to have this feature than older models.
- Turn off your space heater when you leave the room or go to bed.
- Have a qualified technician clean your furnaces and other heating equipment, including chimneys once a year.
- Fit your fireplace with the proper screen to prevent sparks from flying into the room.

ELECTRICAL

Thirteen percent of house fires start because of some type of electrical malfunction in electrical wiring, lamps, cords, plugs or power supplies. Here are some ways you can prevent electrical fires from starting in your home:

- If you have an older home, hire an electrician to inspect your electrical wiring. Many homes built in the 1960s and 1970s have aluminum wiring instead of the safer copper wiring.
- If you are doing a home improvement project, have a qualified electrician help you with wiring.
- Loose-fitting or worn outlets should to be replaced. If a wall plate is broken or missing, replace it so wiring is not exposed.
- If an outlet or switch feels warm, ask an electrician to take a look. Do the same for fuses that blow repeatedly and flickering lights.
- Always plug major appliances directly into the wall. Do not use extension cords.
- Don't overload your extension cords and only use them as a temporary option. Extension cords are not made to be permanent household wiring.
- Avoid running extension cords under furniture or rugs.

BE READY QUICK TIP!

Do you know that 9-volt battery you tossed in the kitchen junk drawer is a fire hazard? If it's out of the packaging, always cover the posts of a 9-volt battery, old or new, with masking, duct or electrical tape. This will prevent the posts from shorting out and starting a fire if they come in contact with metal.

- Repair or replace frayed, tattered worn out electrical cords on appliances and electronics equipment.
- When you replace the light bulbs in your lamps and light fixtures, use the correct wattage.

SMOKING

Cooking is the leading cause of house fires but smoking is the leading cause of house fire deaths. And the smokers are not the only ones dying. One in four victims killed in smoking-related house fires is a non-smoker and a third of those are children. The best ways to prevent smoking related house fires are:

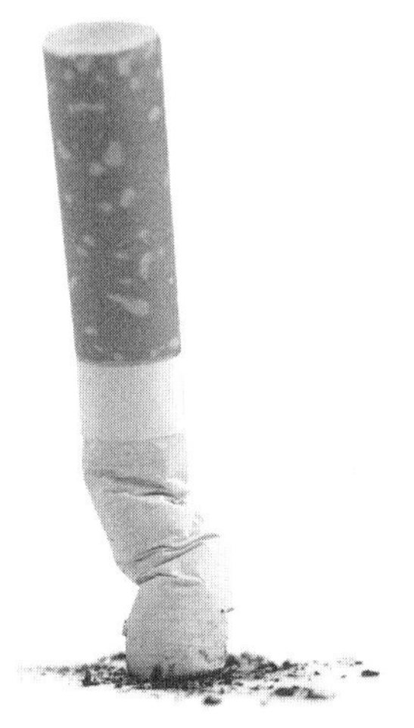

- Smoke outside.
- Always use a heavy, deep ash tray on a sturdy table or a can filled with sand for ashes.
- Douse butts and ashes with water to make sure they are out before you throw them away.
- Don't smoke if oxygen is being used in your home.
- Check for cigarette butts on the floor and under furniture cushions if someone has been smoking inside.
- You need to be alert to prevent fires so never smoke when you are drowsy, drinking or taking medication that makes you sleepy.
- Never smoke in bed.
- Consider smoking fire-safe cigarettes.
- Always have your lighter set on low flame.
- Give up smoking.

APPLIANCES

Right after my husband and I married, we rented an apartment from a landlord who insisted we never run appliances when we weren't home. At the time, we thought it was a little overkill but come to find out appliances—especially clothes dryers—are common causes of house fires. Our landlord had the right idea. Never leave the dryer, washing machine or dishwasher running unattended. Turn them off when you leave the house to run errands or when you are going to bed. Here are some other ways you can prevent appliance-related house fires:

- Three prong cords need to be fitted into three prong outlets. Never force a three prong cord into a two prong extension cord.
- Register your new appliances with the manufacturer so you can be kept up-to-date on safety recalls.
- Clean the dryer's lint trap after every load.
- Use an air canister or vacuum to clean your bathroom exhaust fan. A build up of lint can cause the motor to overheat and start a fire.
- Don't leave your bathroom exhaust fan running longer than necessary or worse, running all day. The fans are designed to run for short periods of time, like during your shower.

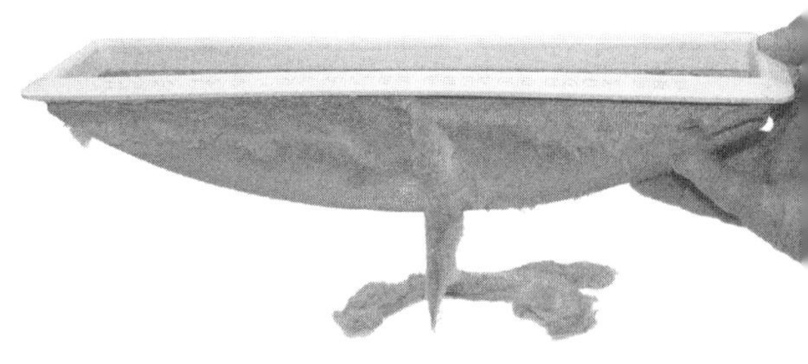

CANDLES

On average, candles are responsible for 42 house fires each day in the United States. As mentioned previously in the chapter on power outages, most candle related fires are preventable if you use common sense. Keep candles away from kids and pets. Don't put them near anything that might catch fire. And if you leave the room, blow them out. Here are some other suggestions for safe candle use:

- Use a candleholder every time. Place it on a stable, heat-resistant surface in an area where it won't be knocked over.
- Always trim the wick to ¼ inch in length before you light it. Doing so prevents uneven burning, dripping and flaring.
- Don't use candles in your bedroom. Thirty five percent of all candle-related fires start where you sleep.

CHILDREN

Every year more than 40,000 house fires are started by children. Preschoolers and kindergarteners are responsible for starting more than half of them. It's never too early to teach kids about the dangers of fire. Talk about how it can hurt them and how fire is hard to control. Establish rules and consequences for playing with fire unsupervised and be ready to follow through. Then, periodically, check under beds and in closets for evidence of fire starting. Kids usually play with fire in hiding places. Here are some additional steps you can take to prevent your children from playing with fire:

- Put matches and lighters up high so they are out of reach. Keep them in a locked container.
- Use child-resistant lighters only.
- Never use lighters or matches to keep a child entertained as a child may mimic your behavior.

BE READY FOR YOUR KIDS TO SLEEP THROUGH **FIRE ALARMS**

Kids sleep through fire alarms. Not too long ago, I woke up in a hotel room to a blaring fire alarm. My preteen daughter did not. You would think the flashing light, deafening buzz and the intercom voice yelling repeatedly, "Please exit now," would have been enough to wake the dead but my daughter never even stirred.

Still not convinced? In a study done by Australia's Victoria University, 78% of the school-age children slept through a fire alarm. It can be easy to forget but children are not mini-adults. Sleeping is one way we're different. Kids spend twice as much time in deep sleep as compared to adults and this stage of sleep is harder to wake from.

I can't stress enough how important it is to practice your fire escape plan at night. Once your family's mastered your home fire escape plan in daylight hours, announce that you will be holding a night time fire drill. Do it the same night as your announcement or inform your family it will be a surprise and will happen sometime during the week. After you've witnessed how your child reacts to a night time alarm, you may need to make adjustments to your fire escape plan. If necessary, assign the task of waking each child to an adult.

Plan For Fires

You can take all the steps to prevent a house fire, but unfortunately, it can still happen. Just in case, I recommend you make a home fire plan. Buy fire safety equipment, develop an escape plan and practice it regularly.

BUY FIRE SAFETY EQUIPMENT

Every home should have fire safety equipment, both to help detect a fire emergency and assist you in dealing with one.

SMOKE DETECTORS

Smoke detectors save lives. Studies have shown that when a house has working smoke detectors, your chance of dying in a fire is reduced by half.

▸ TYPES

Battery-powered smoke detectors are available as well as detectors that are hard-wired to a house's electrical system. There are also detectors that are hard-wired with a battery backup. When you're shopping for smoke detectors, you will see two terms mentioned: ionization and photoelectric. This refers to the type of smoke detection technology. Ionization smoke detectors are the most common. They give an earlier warning to flaming fire than photoelectric smoke detectors, which are quicker to detect a slow, smoldering fire. For the best protection have both types of smoke detectors in your home or choose an alarm that combines both technologies into one unit, called dual sensor smoke alarms.

▸ INSTALL

The size of your home will determine how many smoke detectors you should

FIREFIGHTERS CAN'T HELP YOU IF THEY CAN'T FIND YOU!

Make sure your house is clearly marked with a house number, visible from all directions, day or night. Choose numbers that are four or more inches high and pick block letters rather than cursive. Also, select a color that contrasts the background they will be mounted on. Prominently display the numbers on both sides of your mailbox and near your front door. Be sure bushes, trees or decorative objects do not hide the house numbers.

have. Install a smoke detector on every level, including your basement. Make sure there is one in every bedroom and outside of all sleeping areas.

Smoke rises so mount detectors on the ceiling or high on a wall. Also, drafts could keep them from working properly so avoid placing them near windows, doors, air returns or ducts.

▸ MAINTAIN

Smoke detectors need to be replaced every 10 years. Can't remember when you bought it? Look on the back of the alarm. There will be a manufacture date stamped on it. Smoke detector batteries need to be replaced every year, or sooner if the alarm chirps. Set a standing date, like New Year's Day or your birthday. For example, in my house, we change batteries when we set our clocks back in the fall. Then test your smoke detectors every month by pressing the test button. If one doesn't respond, replace it.

ARE YOUR MEMORIES **ZQUAREDAWAY?**

If your house was on fire and you could only save one thing, what would it be? For many of us, the answer is family photos.

Roberta Flood witnessed first hand the devastation that comes with losing precious family photos when a friend lost a multitude of family albums in a house fire. Flood, a former Army aviator, knew of a material called Nomex that's used to make protective gear for military pilots and firefighters. She had an idea. If Nomex is good enough to protect a life in a fire, then why not use it to protect a family's most valuable possessions?

Flood developed ZquaredAway—firefighter gear for what you hold dear. These fire-resistant protective covers were independently tested and proven to withstand a fire up to 900°F for more than 30 minutes plus the water from firefighter hoses afterwards. They are available in five sizes—the smallest holds four thumb drives and the largest holds multiple photo albums, up to 13x13 inches in size. Lighter and less cumbersome than a fire-resistant safe, ZquaredAway covers provide an attractive and versatile fire-resistant option for your family treasures (and for your Grab and Go Binder!). Available at www.zquaredaway.com.

Dust and other contaminants can affect the detector's ability to sense a fire so it's important to keep it clean. Using your vacuum cleaner's wand attachment, vacuum around the outside of the alarm and then follow the manufacturer's instructions for cleaning the interior.

Avoid painting your smoke detectors when you paint your ceilings. And as cool as those glow in the dark stars are, don't let your kids stick stickers on the detectors. Paint, stickers and other decorations could prevent the detectors from working properly.

Finally, never disable a smoke detector. If it is constantly giving off false alarms, it may be too close to your bathroom or kitchen. Try relocating it. If that doesn't help, it could be a faulty detector. In that case, replace it.

→ FIRE EXTINGUISHERS

It's a good idea to have at least one fire extinguisher for each floor of your home but make sure you have one in the kitchen and the garage, the two areas most susceptible to fire. Also, keep them in a place where they are easily accessible. Mounted next to an exit door is much better than tucked away in a hall closet.

▶ TYPES

Fire extinguishers for homes fall into one of three classes—A, B, or C. If the fire involves ordinary combustibles such as paper, wood, cloth, rubber and plastics, use a Class A fire extinguisher. Use Class B fire extinguishers for fires involving flammable liquids such as gasoline, grease, oil and oil-based paints. Class C fire extinguishers put out fires involving anything that's plugged in—appliances, tools, or electrical equipment. Or, you can opt for the multi-purpose Combination A-B-C fire extinguisher, which would work well for most homeowner's needs.

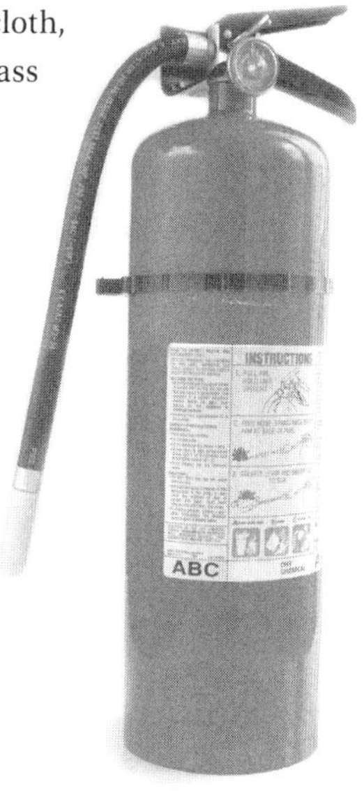

▶ USE

Fire extinguishers have a limited amount of discharge time so you will only have seconds (about ten to 20) to try to put a fire out. To avoid injury, don't even consider using a fire extinguisher if...

- You don't know how to use it. You won't have time to read the instructions.

- You're not physically able to use it. If it's too heavy to hold, it will be too difficult to operate.
- The fire is large and growing. Use it if the fire is small and contained, like in a wastebasket; otherwise let the firefighters handle it.
- You haven't alerted everyone in your family to the fire and called the fire department. A safe escape is more important than putting out the fire.
- The room is filled with smoke. Fire extinguishers have no affect on smoke so it's better to get out than to try and put out.
- You're instincts are telling you it's not safe. Listen to your gut.

▸ MAINTAIN

How often you replace your fire extinguisher depends on whether you have a disposable or a rechargeable model. Disposable extinguishers, the ones with a plastic head and a pressure gauge marked Full and Empty, should be replaced every twelve years. The extinguishers with the metal head and a gauge marked Charge and Recharge are the rechargeable models. These extinguishers need to be refilled every ten years.

Regardless of the model, give it a thorough maintenance check every year. Look over the canister for rust, dents, cracked hoses or broken parts. Read the pressure gauge. If it says anything other than Full or Charge, replace or recharge as necessary.

→ HOME SPRINKLERS

Sprinkler systems are no longer just for commercial buildings. Home fire sprinkler systems are aesthetically pleasing, fast acting and reliable. They are designed to contain or extinguish a fire and cause less water damage than firefighter hoses. While it is possible to retrofit an existing home with a sprinkler system, it's easier to have one installed if you're in the process of building a house.

HOW TO USE A **FIRE EXTINGUISHER**

Remember the word PASS:

- PULL the pin. Remove the pin to unlock the handle.
- AIM low. Point the nozzle at the base of the fire not at the smoke or flames.
- SQUEEZE the trigger. Do it slowly and use even pressure.
- SWEEP side to side. Hit all sides of the fire.

→ PORTABLE FIRE ESCAPE LADDERS

Portable fire escape ladders provide a way out of second and third story windows. If you live in a multi-story home, a portable fire escape ladder is a must have. Store one in an accessible location in each upper level bedroom. Before you purchase a ladder, measure your window sill to ensure the one you select will fit. Then figure out what length you will need. Standard size ladders are 15 and 25 feet long. Buy a ladder that has been evaluated by the safety certification company, Underwriter Laboratories (UL) and can be used more than once.

→ FIRE RESISTANT SAFES

Fireproof is a term that gets used a lot when talking about safes but the reality is no safe is truly fireproof. If exposed to high enough temperatures for an extended period of time, the contents in every safe will be destroyed.

Typically, house fires burn at 800 to 1200°F at peak levels and it takes firefighters 15 to 30 minutes to contain the fire so safes are tested for these conditions before going to market. Underwriter Laboratories (UL) performs independent testing and assigns a rating to a safe based on the item it's protecting and how long it will protect it. Two common ratings you'll see when you are shopping are UL 125 and UL 350.

▸ UL 125

If you see UL 125 marked on a safe or its packaging, it means during a one hour test at 1700°F, the safe's interior temperature did not get higher than 125°F. If you have thumb drive files, CDs or DVDs you're trying to protect, you will want to use an UL125 rated safe. Although the interior still heats up, it doesn't reach 140°F which is the temperature necessary to cause computer data and media to melt.

▸ UL 350

Safes rated UL 350 are best for storing paper, like wills, birth certificates and other documents. Paper chars at around 400°F but during a one hour test at 1700°F, the interior temperature of a UL 350 safe never exceeded 350°F.

Both UL 125 and UL 350 safes are available with temperature protection for a half hour, one hour or two hour. Thirty minute protection is the most common and is usually sufficient as statistics show, on average, it takes firefighters 15 to 30 minutes to contain a fire. But if you would feel more secure with increased protection time, that's fine. Just realize the retail price of the safe increases, too.

PLAN AN ESCAPE

According to the National Fire Protection Association, once the smoke detector alarm sounds, you have as little as two minutes to get out of your home safely. Developing a house fire escape plan in advance of a house fire emergency will help everyone escape quickly. Get everyone involved in the planning. Even the kids. Now is the time to bounce ideas off of one another and ask questions.

Draw the floor plan of your home, including all the doors and windows. Go room to room and figure out two ways to escape. Draw the routes on the map. Next, check all the windows and doors to make sure they open easily. Can your children open them without your assistance?

Then sit down together and review the plan. Where is the outside the home meeting place? Does everyone understand what they should do if there's a fire? Talk to your little ones about how important it is not to hide from firemen. If there's a chance they could be afraid of firefighters, call your local fire department and set up a meeting so your kids have the chance to see firemen dressed in their full protective gear. Lastly, if there is a family member with a disability that would prevent him from escaping on his own, assign someone to help.

PRACTICE

The good news is 71% of us have a fire escape plan. The bad news is less than half of us have actually practiced it. If you're thinking it can't be that hard to get out of the house, remember your house can look very different when it's filled with smoke. Plus in any emergency situation, panic creeps in and tries to take over, making it difficult to stop and think. When you practice your plan regularly, you take thinking out of the equation, which leads to quicker action.

Before you schedule any home fire drills, be sure your family is familiar with all aspects of the house fire escape plan. Start by pushing the test button to set off the smoke detectors. Everyone in the house needs to recognize the sound. Do your children know where the fire escape ladders are located? Are they able to set one up on their own? Choose a first story window and together practice opening the window and screen, hooking the ladder on the sill and throwing the steps out the window. Have your children climb in and out with your assistance until you are confident they will be able to do it on their own. Does everyone know how to use the fire extinguisher? If you have a fire extinguisher that's about to expire take it out into the backyard and practice using it. Does everyone understand if their clothes catch on fire, running away will make it worse? Practice STOP, DROP and ROLL. Stop moving. Drop to the ground. Roll over and over to put the flames out.

Then twice a year conduct home fire drills. To help you remember to do it, schedule your drills in the spring and fall on the same days you change your clocks. Run your drills during the daytime and try to make them as real as possible. What would happen if one of the main exits was blocked? How about more than one? After each drill, hold a family meeting and discuss how it went. What worked? What should be done differently next time? As soon as you feel like everyone has a good handle on the daytime drills, conduct nighttime drills.

It's a House Fire! Now What?

As soon as you hear the smoke detector alarm your one and only goal should be to get out safely. Before you open any door, touch it with the back of your hand. Don't use your palm. If the door is hot and your palm gets burned, your hand won't be usable. If the door is cool, open it slowly. If there is fire or heavy smoke on the other side, shut it and use your secondary exit. If you're trapped, tuck a blanket or clothes in the crack under the door to keep the smoke out. Cover the air vents. Then hang a sheet out the window or use a flashlight to signal firefighters for help.

Once you are outside, go straight to the family meeting place. Call 911. Wait for everyone in your family to arrive. As difficult as it is, don't go back inside for any reason. If someone is missing, tell the firefighters when they arrive. They have the protective equipment needed for performing rescues.

Carbon Monoxide

Sometimes called "the silent killer", carbon monoxide is an odorless, tasteless, poisonous gas that is produced when fossil fuel, like gasoline, propane, oil, and natural gas burns incompletely. The most common household producers of carbon monoxide are cooking and heating equipment, appliances, generators, cars and lawn care equipment. Carbon monoxide isn't something to take lightly. According to the Centers for Disease Control and Prevention, it's responsible for more than 20,000 trips to the emergency room and more than 400 deaths each year.

PREVENT

The number one way to prevent carbon monoxide emergencies is to install and use fuel-burning appliances and equipment properly. Always follow the manufacturer's installation and safety recommendations. For further protection, you should:

- Hire a qualified technician to inspect and clean your heating equipment and chimney every year.
- Make sure the chimney flues are open before you use the fireplace.
- Don't leave cars or lawn mowers running in the garage, even if the garage door is open.
- Never use your gas oven, cooktop or clothes dryer to heat your home.
- Always use your grill outside.
- Set up your generator outside and away from the house.

EQUIPMENT

Carbon monoxide detectors are the best way to alert you to the deadly gas' presence. Buy battery-powered detectors that have met the Underwriter Laboratory's strict standards and are marked UL next to the phrase "Single Station Carbon Monoxide Alarm". Install one detector outside of sleeping areas and be sure you have at least one detector on each level of your home.

Maintaining a carbon monoxide detector is similar to maintaining a smoke detector. Test it once a month and be sure to replace batteries once a year. Every five to seven years buy a replacement. If you're not sure of the age of your detector, look for the manufacture date on the back.

WHAT DO I DO IF THE CARBON MONOXIDE ALARM GOES OFF?

If the carbon monoxide detector alarm sounds, turn off all fuel-burning equipment and open windows and exterior doors to ventilate the house. Get everyone outside into fresh air immediately. Check to see if anyone in your family is experiencing CO poisoning symptoms—headache, dizziness, nausea, sleepiness, breathing difficulty or confusion. Then call 911.

Don't go back into the house until the air is clean. Have a qualified technician inspect your appliances. Once the source of the carbon monoxide is found, do not operate the equipment or appliance until it has been repaired.

HOUSE FIRE EVACUATION PLAN

Create your House Fire Evacuation Plan in the space below. Draw the floor plan of your home, including all the doors and windows. Plan two escape routes from each room and mark them on the map. Make note of the location of all smoke detectors and fire extinguishers as well as the location of your family meeting spot outside of your home.

CHAPTER 11

Home Invasions

According to the Federal Bureau of Investigation, a burglary occurs every 14.6 seconds across the United States. What can you do to be sure your home isn't next? **Make your home an unlikely target.** Burglars are opportunists. They look for homes they believe can be broken into easily without a risk of being caught. Implementing several layers of home security is the best way to make your home look less appealing to crooks.

Doors

Doors are the most common entry point. Most burglars will kick in the door rather than spend time picking the lock. That's why a durable exterior door is important. Solid core doors, made out of wood or metal, are the best choice. Hollow core doors are made for interior rooms and are meant for privacy, not security. All it would take is a good kick and the bad guy gets through. Also, doors with a window or glass side panels within 40 inches of a lock are less secure. It's too easy to smash the glass and reach through to unlock the door.

LOCKS

Locks are no good unless used. Too many of us leave our doors unlocked, giving crooks an open invitation to rob us. Lock your doors when you leave your house, even if you're only stepping out back to do yard work. Keep your doors locked when you're inside your home as well. Robberies have happened while homeowners were in the shower or in another part of the house.

Door knob locks alone do not provide adequate security. The latches are too short and won't hold up if someone kicks the door. Also, once the latch is extended, it can be pushed back. Most amateur burglars are skilled at jimmying the door open by inserting a credit card or screwdriver between the latch and the strike plate (the piece of metal attached to the door frame).

To increase home security, add a deadbolt lock to all exterior doors. Deadbolt locks have a solid bar, called a throw that slides into a hole in the door frame. Once extended the throw can't be pushed back, making it impossible to jimmy the door open. A good deadbolt will have a throw that is a minimum of one inch in length. The cylinder—the outer casing that holds the locking mechanism—should be beveled and made of case-hardened steel to make it more difficult for a crook to hit or twist the lock off with tools. There are even drill-resistant deadbolts and deadbolts with

hacksaw-resistant throws.

If you have a door with window within reaching distance of your deadbolt, you may be tempted to use a double cylinder deadbolt. Double cylinder deadbolts have a key slot on both sides. In order to unlock the door from the inside, you need a key. While this seems like way to improve security, think of the fire safety risk. Will you be able to find and operate a key when you are in a panic or overcome by smoke? Will your kids be able to?

Finally, it's important to note, not all locks are created equal when it comes to quality. While you are shopping, look for a lock that has an ANSI grade 1 security rating, the highest quality rating of the American National Standards Institute.

DOOR HARDWARE

Standard strike plates and hinges usually come with short screws that attach the hardware to the door frame. If a burglar kicks at it, the door frame easily splinters. Replace the short screws with 2 ½ to 3 inch screws. Longer screws will go through the doorframe and into the studs, which will strengthen the frame. You can strengthen the frame even more by replacing the standard strike plate with a heavy duty, four-screw, strike plate.

You never want to open a door without knowing who is on the other side so if your door doesn't already have a peephole, add one. Some doors have safety chains allowing you to open the door a few inches to see who is there. Peepholes are a safer option than a flimsy door chain because once you open the door, it doesn't take much for a bad guy to slide his shoulder in the opening and snap the chain.

Windows

Chances are if a burglar isn't entering your home through a door, he'll be entering through a window. The simplest way to secure your windows is to keep them closed and locked, especially at night while you're asleep. Don't assume it's safe to leave windows open on the second level. Burglars have been known to climb ladders, trees, and even parked cars to gain access to the top floor. Also, be sure window air conditioners are properly secured. It doesn't take much to push a poorly installed air conditioner out of the way. You may want to invest in a steel protective cage for your unit just to be safe.

There are a variety of ways to reinforce your windows. If you have double hung windows, invest in window pins or extra locks to make them difficult to pry open.

Consider replacing standard glass with glass that is designed for added security, like tempered glass, laminated glass or polycarbonate. Invisible security film is another option. Applied to the window, the film will not prevent the glass from breaking. But it will hold the pieces in place, which makes it challenging for someone to crawl through. Whatever method of reinforcement you use, make sure it doesn't interfere with your family's fire escape plan. For example, window bars are the best way to secure your windows. If a burglar smashes the glass he's won't be able to squeeze through the bars to get inside. While this security measure is effective at preventing bad guys from getting in, it also prevents your family from getting out during a fire.

ARE YOU MAKING THESE **HOME SECURITY MISTAKES?**

- You keep a spare key hidden under a doormat, flower pot, or fake rock.
- You ignore your barking or growling dog instead of getting up to investigate.
- You put your last name on your mailbox, making it easy for a crook to look you up and call to see if your home.
- You keep ladders and other tools a burglar can use to gain access to your home laying around your yard.
- You leave a note for the UPS man on your front door when you're not home.
- You forgot to have the locks changed when you moved into your new home.
- You leave the large boxes your expensive new purchases came in on the curb for trash day instead of breaking them down and putting them in the trash can.
- You leave your blinds open at night, making it easy for a burglar to stand at a distance, undetected in the dark, and scope out your house.
- You think because there's a Neighborhood Watch program, it's safe to leave your doors unlocked and your garage open.
- You decide not to call police after the man with the strange story rang your doorbell.

Q: WHEN IS IT SAFE TO LEAVE MY CHILD HOME ALONE?

A: Unfortunately, there is no clear answer. However, before you leave your child home alone, there are some things for you to consider. Some states have child neglect laws stating the minimum age a child can be left home alone but most just offer guidelines. Check with your local child protective services agency for specifics. If your child meets the age set in the guidelines, it still might not be safe to leave them home alone. Ask yourself some questions to determine your child's home alone readiness. Is my neighborhood safe? How secure is my home? Does my child know how to lock all the doors and windows? Can he arm and disarm the alarm? Does he know what to do if the alarm goes off?

Talk to your child about what he should do if someone rings the doorbell. In general, it's best to advise him not to answer the door. And if your child answers the telephone while you're away, make sure he knows never to say you aren't there. Instead, instruct him to say something like "My parents are too busy to come to the phone right now, can I take a message."

Even if you're confident your home is secure and you developed a family plan for home invasions, your child is not ready to be left home alone if...

- Your child is afraid to be left home alone.
- Your child doesn't follow rules and make good decisions.
- Your child doesn't have at least two contacts he can call if he can't reach you.
- Your child doesn't have a safe place—usually a neighbor's home—he can go to if he needs help.
- You child doesn't know how and when to dial 911.
- Your child hasn't been trained on what to do in a fire emergency.
- Your child doesn't know basic first aid.
- Your child doesn't know what to do in the event of severe weather.
- Your child doesn't know how to operate the microwave, toaster oven or stovetop safely.

Garage Doors

Every year or so, I receive an email from the police department notifying the residents of my neighborhood about a rash of garage break-ins. Truth be told, it's not really a break-in as much as it is a walk-in since in every case, the garage doors were left open. The crooks walked right in and helped themselves to tools, golf clubs and more. Unfortunately, this is common in neighborhoods everywhere that's why it's important to keep your garage door closed.

A closed garage doesn't necessarily guarantee a secure garage either. Some thieves will break into cars parked in driveways and use the garage door remotes to gain access to garages. Whenever you park outside the garage, don't leave the garage door remote clipped to the visor. If you don't think you can remember to take it in and out of the car, use a keychain garage door remote instead.

If a burglar succeeds at getting into your garage, do you really want him to be able to waltz right into your house? Treat the entry door from the garage to your house like an exterior door. Install a solid core door with a deadbolt and keep it locked. It's also a good idea to install a peephole in the door. If you hear a noise in the garage, it's safer to investigate through a peephole than it would be to open the door.

When you go on vacation, lock your garage door. Unplugging the garage door opener is one way to do this, however I recommend you physically lock the door with a garage door lock to prevent fishing. Fishing is when burglar slides a hooked coat hanger under the overhang and pulls the emergency release cable to open the door.

Sliding Glass Doors

Sliding glass doors are the most difficult entry point to secure. It's rare that a crook will smash a huge pane of glass since the noise may attract unwanted attention. Nevertheless, apply invisible security film to the glass just in case. To prevent the burglar from busting the lock and sliding the door open, lay a wooden dowel in the track. Also, install several, large pan-head screws into the upper channel to prevent someone from lifting the door out of the track.

Lights

Lighting is a simple and inexpensive way to deter burglars. Exterior lights illuminate the shadows bad guys love to hide in and interior lights can trick them into thinking you are home.

EXTERIOR LIGHTS

Exterior lights should always be turned on at night. Every door should have a light and preferably a two light bulb fixture in case one blows out. Motion sensor lights provide a bright sudden burst of light when someone walks by and can be effective at scaring away someone who is up to no good. At the same time they give you a heads up that someone is in the yard. Install one on all the corners of your house. Be sure it's high out of reach so that a criminal can't unscrew the bulbs or cut wires to disable the light.

INTERIOR LIGHTS

Do you leave a light on when you are away from home? Most of us do. But do you always leave the same light on, like the light over the kitchen sink or the lamp in the corner of the living room? Unfortunately, leaving these "beacon lights" on aren't fooling the crooks. You need to be more unpredictable if you want the bad guys to think someone is home. Put your lights on timers. It is the best way to achieve unpredictability. Timers allow you to randomly turn on lights at scheduled times through the night. Remember, be unpredictable. Avoid scheduling the same light to go at the same time every night.

Landscaping

Remember, the last thing a burglar wants is to be seen. Houses with plenty of hiding places are ideal targets because they keep bad guys from being seen by the neighbors. Take a good look at your home's exterior and eliminate these hiding places. Trim bushes and hedges closest to your driveway, sidewalks, and doors to a height of no more than three feet. Don't let the shrubs under the windows grow taller than the window sill. Prune the lower branches of trees. A good height is seven feet off the ground. Then prune the upper branches away from the house to discourage someone from climbing the tree to gain access to your second story.

Some homeowners believe fencing will deter a burglar because he can't walk through the yard as easily. This is true but fences—especially privacy fencing—provide cover for bad guys since they can make it difficult for neighbors to see your house. If you have a fence, be sure to keep the gate closed and locked.

Landscaping can be used to deter someone from breaking in. Plant thorny shrubbery like barberries, roses or yucca under your windows and along fences.

GOING ON **VACATION?**

Burglars are on the lookout for unattended homes, so before you leave on a family trip, do your best to secure your home. If you've been meaning to install that deadbolt but just haven't gotten around to it yet, get it done before you leave on vacation. Put your lights on timers and don't forget to activate your alarm when you leave.

Inform your neighbors of your plans so they can keep watch on your house. Make arrangements for them to pick up your mail and put your trash cans out on trash day. If it's winter, make arrangements for snow removal. Pristine white snow on the driveway and walkways is a dead giveaway that no one is home. If you can't rely on your neighbors consider hiring a house sitter. You can also stop mail and newspaper delivery through the post office and newspaper. It is better than leaving it to pile up but understand that you are still taking a chance. You just don't know who is privy to the stop request information.

Check with your police department. Do they offer vacation security checks? In my town, homeowners can inform the police department of vacation plans. During their absence, a police officer will periodically stop by the home to check for open doors, broken windows or any other sign of a break-in.

Keep quiet about your vacation plans on social media. Posts like "Paris, here we come!" on your Facebook page are not the best idea. Yes, you may have the privacy settings activated but how well do you really know everyone on your friends list? Save the vacation photos and the status updates for when you return. Also, avoid talking about your vacation plans in public. It's very possible that the wrong person will overhear you. They may decide to follow you home to see where you live and then come back and rob you while you are away.

Place gravel on the ground in front of first story windows. It's difficult for the bad guys to sneak around when they are making loud crunching footsteps.

Lastly, a well-maintained lawn and landscape can also be a psychological deterrent. If you take the time to keep the exterior of your home in tip-top shape, you are sending a message that you care about your home and a burglar may assume you've taken steps to protect it.

Dogs

Dogs are a great addition to your home security plan. Not all dogs are intimidating but most provide another security layer a potential thief has to get through. Once the burgular realizes he will have to deal with a dog, he will usually pass up your house in favor of dog-free home.

Most dogs make good watch dogs. Their barking alerts you to potential invaders. And if properly trained, some dogs are excellent protection dogs and can be relied on to keep you or your property safe from an intruder. Before you add a dog to your home, do your homework. There are breeds that have stronger protective or territorial instincts. Read up on different breeds, visit animal shelters and seek the advice of a good dog trainer.

If you already have a dog, be realistic about his home security abilities. Will he warm up quickly to someone with treats? Does he cower from strangers? Or does he happily greet everyone who comes through the door? You hope he will jump into protection mode when there's a threat, but you can't be sure. His behavior may not be different with a burglar. On the other hand, an aggressive dog that would surely hurt an intruder isn't necessarily the best answer either. There is always a risk he could hurt a friend or family member.

If an alarm system isn't in your budget, keep your car keys beside your bed at night. Hear a noise? Hit the panic button on the key fob to set off the car alarm. There's a good chance the noise will scare the burglar away.

Neighbors

Who keeps an eye on your home when you're away? Get to know your neighbors. I have an agreement with my next door neighbors on both sides to watch each other's houses when we go on vacations. It's great to have someone pick up the mail, turn on lights and take out the trash—all the things that help keep up that lived-in appearance. And it's comforting to know that if something suspicious is going on, one of them will immediately call the police. I highly recommend you build a support network with the people on either side of your home and those across the street if you feel they could be trustworthy.

Neighborhood Watch programs are another way neighbors helping neighbors effectively lower the risk of home burglaries. The purpose of a watch group is not to act as police. Instead, neighbors agree to be alert to their surroundings and report suspicious activity if they see it. If your neighborhood doesn't already have a program you can join, consider starting one. Find like-minded neighbors who are willing to commit the time. Then contact your police department and ask for their assistance in forming the group.

Alarm Systems

No home is 100-percent burglar-proof but research shows that a home with a good alarm system is less likely to get broken into than one without. For some crooks, it's the fear of getting caught, for others it's the hassle of dealing with another security layer.

The best alarm system is a monitored one. The alarm is connected to a central monitoring station and if it's activated, someone is there to notify the police. The only downfall is it's not cheap. You'll pay for the equipment, installation and then a monthly monitoring fee. How much you're willing to invest will determine what options are available to you. Some options are: motion detectors, glass break detectors, video surveillance cameras, panic buttons, flood detectors, battery back-up, remote control key fobs and fire and carbon monoxide alarms. Usually, signing a two or three year monitoring contract with the company results in a hefty discount on the price of equipment and there's no shortage of companies offering systems. It pays to shop around. Do some research and go with a reputable company.

If you've made the investment, use it. There's only been two break-ins on my street since I've lived here. In both cases, the homeowners forgot to turn on their alarms. Too many of us don't activate our alarms because we forget, we decide not to or we don't even know how. Your alarm system is useless if it isn't turned on. Teach everyone in your house how to arm and disarm the system and make setting the alarm a house rule.

Home Invasions

I've always said, "If you are going to break into my house, please do it when I'm not home."

As bad as burglaries are, home invasions are worse. A home invasion is when a criminal forces his way into your house while you are home with the intent of stealing from or harming you. Home invasions are terrifying and in some cases deadly.

PREVENTION

There are things you can do to reduce the chance of a home invasion. Keep exterior doors locked and if you have one, turn on your alarm system when you are home. Yes, it's inconvenient and no, it won't prevent someone from entering your home. But it will give you advance warning of an intruder and as a result you will have more time to react. At the same time, it will notify authorities that you need help.

If the doorbell rings and it's someone you don't know, always assume they are there to do you harm. Never open the door! Instead, talk to them through the door. I'll admit when I first started doing this, I felt pretty stupid. But you will get used to it (I promise!) and frankly, who cares. Your safety is more important than what the other person thinks.

If the person on the other side of the door needs help and is asking to use your phone, offer to make the call for them instead. And don't be tricked into opening the door by someone is dressed as a pizza delivery or repairman. If you are expecting a repairman, don't assume that the person ringing the bell is him and fling the door wide open. Again, ask through the closed door who is there. If the person says they are from a utility company but you aren't expecting them, place a call to the utility company and find out if they are who they say they are.

If you absolutely can not get used to the idea of talking to someone through the door, I recommend you only open it a little ways. Brace your shoulder and your foot against the back of the door so it will be harder to push past you.

Finally, be aware of what's going on in your neighborhood so you will know if something doesn't seem right. Is there a strange car parked within view of your house? Report anything out of the ordinary to the police. And if you pull into your neighborhood and see that the same car has been behind you since you left the grocery store, do not pull into your driveway. Pass by and go somewhere public, like a store or restaurant, and call the police.

SAFE ROOMS

Whenever I hear the word safe room, images of a high-tech steel fortress similar to Jodie Foster's in the movie *Panic Room* comes to mind. Some homeowners actually have fortified safe rooms, but if you don't, you can make a simple, effective one.

Choose a room away from entry doors. A windowless, interior room works best, like a bathroom or closet. When considering your options think about how the room will work for your family. Do you have small children? If so, their bedroom closet may make the perfect safe room since you'll be running to get them anyway. Is your bedroom on a different level than your children's? Maybe you need to create two safe rooms—one upstairs and one downstairs—in case it's impossible for everyone to get together in time.

Once you've chosen the room, get busy reinforcing it. Replace the door with a solid core door. Throw away your flimsy interior door knob and use one made for exterior doors. Add a deadbolt to the door. (Two is fine too!) Strengthen the strike plate by using longer screws. Mount hinges (with non-removable pins) on the outside, so the door swings out instead of in. This will make it more difficult to kick in. And don't forget the peephole! Whatever room you choose, the goal is to put as many barricades as possible between you and the intruder. If you choose a bedroom closet, it's not a bad idea to double your protection and fortify the bedroom door too.

Your safe room should be equipped with a way to call 911. If you don't keep your cell phone within arms reach 24/7, then run a landline into the room. Another option is to get a spare cell phone and store it, fully charged, in the room. Make sure you add a flashlight, first aid kit and a weapon.

WEAPONS

When we hear the word weapon, most of us think of guns. Before you bring a firearm into your home, ask yourself these questions:

- Are you willing to take a life to protect you or your family and then cope with the life-changing consequences?
- Are you able to responsibly and safely handle, use and store a gun?

- Are you willing to receive proper training?

If you answer no to any of these questions, then skip right over this section. It's OK if guns are not for you. Instead, a more suitable weapon might be a Taser, pepper spray, or my former pre-gun favorite, a baseball bat.

→ GUN LAWS

If you're thinking of becoming a gun owner, learn your state's gun laws. A state-by-state summary is available on the National Rifle Association's website at www.nraila.org/gun-laws/state-laws.aspx. And since these laws change, you'll need to stay informed. Be sure you are clear on the laws regarding the use of deadly force. You can't take a bullet back. Once you've fired a gun, you have to live with the consequences.

→ SAFETY AND HANDLING

Responsible gun owners practice safe handling rules every single time they pick up a gun—no exceptions. Always treat a gun as if it's loaded. Always point the gun in a safe direction. Always keep your finger off the trigger until you're ready to shoot. And lastly, always identify what you are shooting at before you shoot (Never shoot at noises!) and know what's behind it.

Before you purchase a gun, do your research to figure out what gun is right for you. Shotguns and handguns are popular choices for home defense but I don't recommend you buy either until you have had the chance to shoot them. Go to a range that offers training courses and try different models and calibers.

Once you purchase a gun, learn how it operates. How do you load and unload it? How do you clear it? How do you clean it? Decide how you will safely store it. Will you carry it holstered on your body at all times? Or will you invest in a gun safe? Once you've come up with a safe storage plan, follow it. Safety is no one else's responsibility but yours.

→ TRAINING

Just because you're willing to take a life to protect your loved ones, doesn't mean you have the cool-headed composure needed to carry it out. Are you sure you will respond quickly and confidently under any circumstances? Or will you hesitate, giving the bad guy a chance to grab your gun and turn it on you or a family member? Invest in shooting lessons with an experienced firearms instructor. You'll learn the fundamentals like proper grip, stance and trigger control before you move onto more advanced skills—quick draw, shooting at moving targets and shooting in low light conditions.

Then, make a commitment to practice regularly. A former Navy Seal friend of my family who is also a firearms instructor once told me: Under extreme stress, we all revert back to our training. If your training consists of one or two sessions at the indoor range shooting at stationary targets, you will probably freeze up and do nothing in a scary situation.

MAKE A HOME INVASION PLAN

It's impossible to predict exactly how an intruder will get in the house and how everyone will react. That's why it's important for your family to sit down together to discuss possible "What if" scenarios and make a plan. What if a bad guy breaks through the door in the middle of the day? What if there are two bad guys? Nothing is too farfetched. Let your imagination run wild.

Another part of your plan should be to come up with a code word. Similar to yelling "Fire", when the code word is used, everyone in the family must react as planned. The plan may be to get to the safe room or it may be to exit the house. And then just like you practice your fire escape plan twice a year, practice your home invasion escape plan.

It's a Home Invasion! Now What?

If you hear glass break or some other commotion, don't go and investigate. Instead, the best thing to do is stay out of the way. Get to your safe room or get out of the house and call 911.

If you wake up and realize there is someone in your house, keep quiet and assess the situation. How many people are there and where are they in your house? Can your family get out of your house safely? If not, get to your safe room and call 911. Drop something heavy on the floor. They may not have known you were home and the noise might scare them away. If the intruder tries to break into your safe room, tell him you already called the police. Then warn him you have a weapon and get ready to fight.

If you can't get out or get to your safe room and you're forced to interact with the intruder, stay calm and do what he says. Hand over any valuables without hesitation. If he turns violent, fight back with everything you got, keeping one goal in mind: escape.

Personal Safety

Not too long ago I was having a conversation with a friend and she said, "Personal safety pretty much never crosses my mind." I'll admit I was a little shocked and a lot concerned. I understood her feeling safe, because statistically, we live in a low-crime area. But let's stop for a second and think about all the news stories we've seen and read about violent crimes. How many times have you heard the victims say, **"I never thought it would happen to me."**

How many times have you seen a witness stand in front of the camera and proclaim, "Stuff like this just doesn't happen around here." No one ever thinks violent crime is going to happen but guess what? It does and it can certainly happen to you.

I'm not suggesting you become some sort of paranoid, worry-wart. What I am suggesting is that you should be able to detect a dangerous situation, do your best to avoid danger, and know how to defend yourself if necessary.

Detect Danger

Once you've swallowed that big pill of reality, the next step is to be able detect when you are facing a potential threat or heading into a dangerous situation. How do you do this? You start by being aware and trusting your instincts.

BE AWARE

Be aware means paying attention to what is happening around you. This advice isn't new and it is usually coupled with something like, "carry yourself with confidence." The idea is that if you do both these things you will look like someone a criminal wouldn't want to mess with and they will pass you over for an easier target.

For the longest time, whenever I would walk through a parking lot, I'd stand up straighter, pull my shoulders back, walk quickly and glance over my shoulders once or twice. I now realize that a quick look left and right and even checking behind you a few times doesn't necessarily mean you are aware.

Being aware is taking everything in. It's like looking at the world through a wide-angle lens. Being aware is using all your senses. It's making mental notes of what you see, hear, smell. It is paying attention to little details and anticipating future actions—both yours and the actions of the people around you.

Walk with me into a Big Box Store parking lot for a moment. As we head toward your car, did you see the father handing shopping bags to his adolescent son who is standing in the bed of a white Chevy pickup truck parked two rows away? What about the blue Honda Accord that has passed you twice while searching for a closer parking spot? Was that a thin middle-aged woman driving it? Did you hear the crash of shopping carts as the gray-haired gentleman pushed his cart into the corral? What's that smell? The employee leaning on the corner of the building is smoking a cigarette and holding a Coke. Did you make eye-contact with the man getting out of the car next to yours? In less than ten seconds, he will be passing by. Have you asked yourself who or what could help if a problem were to arise? Did you notice the smoking employee throw the butt on the top of the trashcan and return to the store? Did you look inside, around and underneath your car as you approached? Did you turn and watch the passing man continue down the aisle?

Whoa, that sounds like a lot of work and too much paranoia. You may think that but it really isn't. We go through our day in various states of awareness. (There are plenty of awareness theories out there, from new age discussions on consciousness to "Cooper's colors," a color- coded system used to train law enforcement and the military.) For our purposes, let's just call these states zoned out, plugged in or focused.

When you are zoned out, your mind wanders. During these times you're lost in your thoughts, or living with your "head in the clouds." Thoughts and daydreams cause us to zone out and so do distractions like cell phones, texting, television, and mp-3 players. How many times have you asked your kids to do something while they're watching TV and they say "What?" There's a good reason for that. Scientists have concluded when you are zoned out, you almost always have no idea what's going on around you. We could have told them that, right?

Plugged in is when you are relaxed and scanning your surroundings. You notice the people and things around you but you're not honed in on anyone or anything in particular. You're looking at the whole picture. You're observing. Driving is a great example of being plugged in. You're not just looking at pavement directly in front of you. You watch the road ahead, the other cars, pedestrians, and anticipate potential hazards. And you're able to do it simultaneously with no fear or tension.

And then there is focused. When you are focused, you are paying full attention. You are on guard because you think it's possible you could be harmed. All your senses are engaged and you are probably tense. Focused is total concentration. Let's look at the driving example again. When you were learning to drive most likely you were focused, rather than just plugged in. Your hands gripped the steering wheel tightly. You slowly rolled up to an intersection and sat there for a minute while you checked three or four times for oncoming traffic. Do you remember that tension you felt? Do you remember checking and re-checking everything you did and everything around you? That's being focused.

It's impossible to stay focused continuously. Yes, it's a little paranoid but more importantly, it's not healthy. Your body isn't capable of handling that level of stress and the adrenaline rush that goes along with it for an extended period. When you are out in public, stay plugged in. This is especially important when you are in familiar surroundings as your mind tends to zone out when it gets comfortable. Notice the things around you and if something doesn't look right, then zoom in and focus. You will appear more confident, reducing your chance of becoming a victim.

→ HOW TO BECOME MORE AWARE

What do you do if you have a hard time staying plugged in? Is there a way to exercise your mind and train it to be more aware? Yes! Luckily, there is.

PLAY MEMORY GAMES

Kim's Game is a fun memory game your whole family can play and it's great for improving awareness. The game is derived from a 1901 adventure novel by

YELLOW JACKET: A SMARTPHONE CASE THAT STINGS

In 2011, Seth Froom was robbed at gunpoint in his home. For weeks after his harrowing ordeal, Froom thought about all the things he could have done to stop the attack. Then he had a light-bulb moment. Since most of us have our smartphones close at hand, Froom thought why not turn an iPhone into a self-defense tool?

Acting on his idea, Froom created the Yellow Jacket, a rugged iPhone case that doubles as a stun gun. Delivering a 650,000-volt shock, the case won't cause permanent harm but it packs enough of a punch to surprise an attacker, giving you an opportunity to escape.

To prevent you from accidentally shocking yourself, the Yellow Jacket has dual safety features—an on/off switch and a protective cover for the electrodes. However, if you hand over your smartphone to your child to pass the time, Yellow Jacket recommends you remove the case first.

Some states ban stun guns so be sure to check your state and local laws before you make a purchase. Yellow Jackets cost around $100. For more information go to www.yellowjacketcase.com.

Rudyard Kipling called Kim. In the book, an orphan named Kim is being trained to become a spy by a British spymaster in 19th Century India. The spymaster introduces Kim to the Play of the Jewels, a memory game we now call Kim's Game. Here's how it works. Collect a variety of objects—coins, colored pencils, Legos, whatever. Fifteen or so, should do it. Spread them out on a tray or table and cover them with a towel. Gather your family around the table and remove the cloth for one minute. Cover the items again and ask everyone to make a list the items they saw. The person who is able to list the most items wins. For a more difficult version of the game, ask everyone to list the items along with identifying details. For example, there are three pencils—red, green, and orange. The orange pencil has a broken tip. The person with the most correct observations wins the game.

Kim's Game doesn't have to be limited to your kitchen table. Take your observation skills out to the streets. When you're out and about with your family, take notice of the people you see. How many are men and how many are women?

PARKING LOT **SAFETY**

A parking garage or lot is an attractive location for bad guys. It's also a place we can't easily avoid, so we need to take extra safety precautions. Here are some things you can do to increase your chance of staying safe:

- Park as close to your destination as possible. Drive around the parking lot once or twice if you have to until you find the right space.
- Park in a well-lit spot and avoid parking near shrubbery or vans with sliding doors.
- Back your car into the parking space when you park. If your car faces out, it will be easier to leave in a hurry if a threatening situation develops.
- Before you get out of your car, take a look around. If anything seems off, don't get out. Drive away.
- Don't leave valuables in plain view in your car.
- Make note of where you park so you won't wander aimlessly later in search of your car.
- Make a plan before you enter the lot. What will you do if you see a potential threat? What will you do if you're attacked?
- Pay attention. Do a continuous 360° scan of the parking lot as you make your way through it. And stay off your cell phone. No exceptions.
- Have your keys in hand before you enter the parking lot. It's impossible to pay

attention to your surroundings when you're rummaging through your purse looking for your keys. Also, carry your cell phone in your pocket, not your purse. If your purse gets ripped off you will still have your phone to call for help.

- Don't forget about the panic button on your key fob. If you feel threatened, use it. The noise may scare off the bad guy.
- Keep as much distance as possible between you and potential hiding places. Walk down the middle of the parking aisle and don't cut in between parked cars.
- If you see something suspicious or if your intuition says something's off, go back into the store or your workplace. Ask someone—a co-worker or store security guard—to walk with you.
- At night, carry a small, high intensity flashlight and use it to help you see threats. Illuminate all the dark areas around and under your car as you approach. Flash the light on your backseat before you unlock and get into the car.
- If you have kids in tow, load your packages first then put your kids in the car. You are most at risk when you are distracted so remain on high alert the whole time and work quickly.
- Once you are in the car, lock the doors and leave. Don't text or make calls. Don't organize your coupons for the next stop. Don't do anything except drive away.

What are they wearing? What are they doing? Drinking coffee? Talking on their phone? Watching you? When you go into a store or restaurant, notice the details. What color are the walls? Where are all the exits? What kind of things could you hide behind? Playing these observations games are a good way to train your mind and before you know it awareness will come naturally.

USE YOUR PERIPHERAL VISION

Right now, as you're reading this, notice the objects in your peripheral vision. Without moving your eyes away from the page, what do you see to the left and right? What do you see above and below? Most of us look at the world with blinders on and never tap into our peripheral vision. Practice monitoring your surroundings out of the corner of your eye. Who knows, one day it may give you the heads up you need to escape a threat approaching from the side.

MEDITATE

Once I committed to being aware, I practice every day while walking on the neighborhood greenway. I tune into the sounds—footsteps, chirping birds, rustling leaves—and breathe in the smells. I see rabbits dart into the underbrush, a black snake sunning himself in the grass next the path and most times, a woman struggling to recapture her unleashed dog. While I take in my surroundings, an amazing thing happens. I am not thinking about what I will make for dinner or how horrible I played in my tennis match that morning. My mind is blank but I am 100 percent engaged without much effort. Meditation will give you the same sensation. When you quiet the chatter in your head and focus on the present moment, it heightens your senses. Set aside time every day to be still. Focus on the rhythm of your breathing. Get used to the feeling of your heightened senses and it will be easier to use them when you need to.

TRUST YOUR GUT

Have you ever been in a situation where you are in a conversation with someone you just met and by all appearances everything seems fine? They look normal and they're saying all the right things but for some reason your stomach is tightening. As it gets harder to breathe, you tell yourself, there's nothing to be afraid of. And because most of us are taught to think instead of feel, you choose to believe that's true and you push that feeling back down to where it came from.

For 20 years, I tuned in to The Oprah Winfrey Show. Over and over again, Oprah interviewed people who had unspeakable things happen to them. In almost every case, each one of these people had a moment before the event where they thought, "Hmmmm, something isn't right." But instead of tapping into the feeling and accepting it as a warning sign, they rationalized it away saying things like "He couldn't possibly do that to me because he loves me" or "I thought I was imagining it."

Your instinct, gut feeling, intuition, hunch, whatever you want to call it, is your built in alarm system. It's your subconscious mind picking up on danger cues without your conscious mind getting in the way. Don't ignore it. If it turns out to be a false alarm, so be it. It's always better to err on the side of safety.

Avoidance

Another way to stay safe in public is to avoid being attacked. Stay away from danger, don't be an easy target and de-escalate, or diffuse, a potentially dangerous situation.

STAY AWAY FROM DANGER

Common sense tells us one of the best ways to prevent becoming a victim of an attack is to avoid behavior, people and places that can get us in trouble. For example, stay away from areas known for higher crime rates. Avoid relationships with people who have violent tendencies. Don't use the stairs in the parking garage and don't use the ATM at night.

It's important to take these precautions and it's also important to realize there are no set rules for staying safe. Avoiding dangerous behavior, people and places will greatly reduce your chance of becoming a victim of a crime, but it's not fool-proof. Never forget that crime has no boundaries. Plus, if you think you are with the right people, in the right place, doing the right thing, you assume there is nothing to worry about. As a result, you pay less attention to what's happening

BE READY QUICK TIP!

Never let yourself be taken to another location. Go ballistic—kick, punch, bite, scream. If you leave with an attacker, you have little chance of making it out alive.

around you. And remember, when you aren't paying attention, you look like an easy target.

DON'T BE AN EASY TARGET

If a predator thinks he won't be successful if he attacks you, he probably won't. Being aware is the best way to look less desirable to the bad guys but here are some more things you can do to be a tough target and reduce the risk of an attack:

- Don't walk alone. It's much harder to attack two people than it is one.
- Stay off the smart phone. Avoid making calls, texting, or emailing while you are out and about.
- If you're heading to the store, leave that expensive purse and all your valuable jewelry at home.
- Be selective about the clothes and shoes you wear in public. The bad guys know that some clothing items—like high heels—will make it harder for you to escape.
- Don't have too much to drink in public.
- Always remain on a high alert when you have your kids in tow.

DE-ESCALATE THE SITUATION

Another method of avoidance is de-escalation. De-escalation is when you sense you are in danger of a physical confrontation, so you speak or act in a way that diffuses the situation. Remember what it was like to be in the grocery store with a toddler on the brink of having meltdown? (We've all been there at least once, right?) You make every effort to stay cool, calm and collected as you change the subject, distract, empathize with, re-focus, and set limits, or just plain listen to the

BE READY QUICK TIP!

Do you know what a gun shot sounds like? If the only shots you've heard were in the movies, take your family to a gun range just to hear the sound. Being able to recognize the sound of gun fire immediately may save your lives one day.

IS YOUR KID A **radKID?**

Take a look at these statistics:

- Physical force is used 85% of the time during child abductions.
- A child is more likely to be a victim of youth violence on school grounds than on the way to school.
- Five percent or 864,000 students admit to staying home from school at least once a month because they are afraid of being harmed.

Alarming, right? One organization thinks so and is committed to doing something about it.

RadKIDS is a non-profit whose mission is to teach, train and empower kids to avoid, resist and escape harm. Certified instructors accomplish this not by telling kids what to do but actually showing them how to do it. Rad stands for resisting aggression defensively and children leave the program with awareness, personal safety strategies, and self-defense skills. In addition to how to fight off an attacker, how to escape and how to call for help, the radKIDs curriculum covers a variety of safety topics like:

- Bullying
- Home and school safety
- Vehicle and bike safety
- Internet safety
- Good, bad and unwanted touch

Concerned this program will scare your kids more? It actually does the opposite. It gives them confidence that they have the power to protect themselves. To find a program near you visit www.radkids.org.

child. If you're skilled enough, before you know it, the tantrum's been averted. That is de-escalation in the truest sense of the word.

One thing to note, in order for de-escalation to work you must let go of the need to be right. The person could be saying or doing the most ridiculous thing you've ever heard but don't try to prove them wrong. This doesn't mean you necessarily have to say they are right, but you should make them feel like you are in agreement.

You also need to be aware of what your body is saying and not just focus on your words. Eye-contact, finger pointing, sighing, shoulder shrugging, or quick-movements have the potential to work against you.

Defending Yourself

When avoidance doesn't work and you find yourself in a full blown physical attack, how do you defend yourself? You fight back.

If you're not a fighter by nature you may be tempted to skip this section. Don't. Fighting back is less about fighting and more about escaping. Use whatever skills or tools are available, thus providing an opportunity to get away. Let's look at tools for fighting back.

SELF DEFENSE SKILLS

To learn self defense skills, enroll in a self-defense class. Self defense classes teach you awareness, assertiveness and physical techniques with a goal of giving you the tools needed to escape, resist or survive an attack. One of the benefits of a self-defense course is a boost in your self-confidence. It's very empowering to be out in public and know that you have knowledge and skills to protect yourself and your children. If you are ever facing an attacker, you won't be thinking, "What was that technique I saw on the Ellen Show?" Plus, you can't argue the fact that a self-defense class is a great workout.

Self defense classes are offered in community centers, colleges, YMCA, private gyms and occasionally they're offered at gun ranges. Check out martial arts studios, too, but realize not all martial arts schools teach practical personal protection strategies that will be helpful in the real world. For more realistic training, consider Krav Maga, an Israeli self-defense system. The bottom line is no two courses are the same. Because of the variety of instructors, techniques and styles, it's best to do your own research to find a course that's right for you.

When you are researching classes, look for a class that offers a variety of options. A good class knows there are no absolutes in self-protection and won't give you a list of "shoulds" and "should nots". A good class will teach you fighting techniques as well as how to analyze a situation. It gives suggestions as to what works in most situations and respects that sometimes the best option is not fighting back.

WEAPONS

Previously we spoke about guns and important things to consider before bringing one into your home as part of your home-security plan. Carrying a gun on your body or in your purse requires the same considerations and then some. You are making a serious decision when you decide to carry and it comes with some huge responsibilities. For example, in addition to the laws pertaining to gun ownership, there are strict laws regarding concealed carry and self-defense. Are you ready to keep current with all of the state and federal laws and get the required permits?

Also, regular training and practice is absolutely essential if you plan to carry. A firearm on your hip will make you feel safer but do you have the tactical skills to support that feeling? Can you access and draw your gun quickly? Now, let's imagine an attacker is close enough to grab you, are you still as confident? Are you sure enough of your skills that your gun won't be turned around and used on you? Or on an innocent bystander?

Finally, carrying a gun requires a certain mindset. It's your responsibility to avoid conflict at all costs. Don't pick fights and always walk away instead of responding to aggressive comments or gestures. If you have trouble keeping your temper in check, you shouldn't carry a gun.

If guns aren't for you, consider pepper spray, a taser, stun guns, knives, tactical pens and key chain weapons. Before you purchase any weapon, always check your local laws to see if it's legal.

WHAT TO DO **IF YOU HEAR GUN SHOTS**

If you are caught in a shooting rampage, there's only one thing for certain. You won't have time to think. Research has shown the average active shooter incident lasts 12 minutes. In that time, law enforcement experts say your options are limited to run, hide or fight. Whatever action you take, do it immediately.

RUN. The moment you hear gun shots, run! Drop your stuff—your purse, shopping bags, anything you're carrying—and head to the nearest exit. You become less of a target the further away you are. If you are close enough to be seen by the shooter, make yourself into a smaller target. Crouch down as you run and get out of his line of sight. Don't stop running until you reach safety. Once you are out of harm's way, call 9-1-1.

HIDE. If you can't escape by running away, hiding is the next best thing. Find cover behind a large solid object like a tree, a planter, a bench, or an ATM machine. The best place to hide is a room with a locking door. Get inside and do what you can to secure the room to keep the shooter out of your hiding place. Shut the lights, lock and barricade the door with furniture. If there's a window, close the blinds. Most importantly, be absolutely silent. (Turn off the ringer to your cell phone!) Stay in your hiding place until the police come and find you.

FIGHT. Fighting should be your last option. If you can't run away or hide, you will have

no other choice but fight. Fight with everything you have and with any improvised weapon you can find. If you are with other people, you may be more successful if you attempt a coordinated attack.

If you carry a gun, you probably have already imagined what you would do in an active shooter situation. If your plan is to take down the shooter, security experts advise against it. While you may be thinking you can't stand by and watch innocent people get killed, do you have the training, tactical skills and experience to engage the shooter in such an extreme situation? Will you be immediately successful at neutralizing the threat or will your attempt just turn his attention to you and your loved ones? Can you be sure you won't hit an innocent bystander? Then there's always the risk that the police will mistake you for the bad guy. The best choice is still run. Use your gun only as a last resort to secure your safety if you can't get away.

From now on, any time you are in a public place, take a second to make a plan. Play the "what if" game. Go through the run-hide-fight sequence. Where will you run to? If you are inside, let's say at a mall for instance, locate the nearest exit in all directions. Where are the possible hiding places? And if necessary, what will you do if you're forced to fight for your life?

CHAPTER 13

Ready Kids are Safe Kids

Soon after my daughter turned 2, I lost her in Super Target. We were standing in the baby section as I decided between two brands of diapers. One minute, my daughter was right there next to me and then she was gone. **A gut twisting, eyes-see-white, panic washed over me.** I tried to hold it together as I ran to the next aisle, screaming her name. She's not there. Teetering on the edge of hysteria, I continued to the next aisle. No luck. As I turned the corner of the third aisle, I saw her. Relief. The crazy instantly went away, although it took me several minutes to catch my breath.

Nothing scares us more than not being able to protect our children. We want to give them the freedom to go out and play without us but deep down, we worry someone may take them if we're not there. We allow them to access the Internet and then we question our decision. How can we be sure who they are talking to? There's a news report of a child accidentally shooting himself and we think what if? We're frustrated when our child tells us he is bullied, but other than taking care of that bully once and for all ourselves, we don't know how to help him handle the situation. In this chapter, let's look at some of those worries—abduction, technology, guns, and bullies—and discuss what we can do to help keep our kids safe.

Abduction

Our fears intensify when we hear of a child snatched off the street but the reality is stranger abductions are rare. In the last nationwide study, out of 800,000 reports of missing kids in one year, a much smaller number, 115, were taken by a stranger. Family members—usually a result of a custody dispute—take far more kids than strangers do. And the vast majority of missing children are lost, abandoned or runaway from home. Also included in the number are kids whose parents report them missing before finding out they were just not where they said they'd be.

Even if there's a low probability your child will be snatched off the street by a stranger, as parents, our job is to educate our kids on how to stay safe. The good news is there are some simple strategies to accomplish this.

DON'T SAY "DON'T TALK TO STRANGERS"

Little ones have a hard time grasping the concept of a stranger. Most children hear the word stranger and imagine someone who is mean and looks scary or dirty. Someone who acts nice and looks normal is not a stranger in their eyes and unfortunately, kidnappers and molesters know this. Many will spiff up their appearance in an effort to lure your child away easier.

Also, teaching your child never to talk to strangers can backfire if one day your child needs the help of a stranger. Imagine what would happen if she's lost in the mall and she won't talk to a policemen or a store clerk.

Finally, the chance your child will be abducted or exploited by a stranger is slim. Seventy-five percent of kidnapped children are abducted by a family member or someone they recognize. Instead of trying to explain who is and who isn't a stranger, focus on teaching your child to watch out for bad adult behavior like inappropriate touching, asking her for help, and telling her to keep secrets.

DEVELOP A PLAN OF ACTION

Developing a plan of action with your kids is the best way to be sure they will know what to do if they're ever approached by a potential predator. Plus it will make them a more difficult target, which could ultimately prevent them from being taken.

The first part of the plan is to create the no-exceptions rule—your child should always ask for your permission before they accept anything or go anywhere with an adult. Be sure they understand if someone asks for them for help, they need to check with you before they lend a hand.

Your children should be taught that keeping secrets is not allowed in your family. In fact, eliminate the word secret from your vocabulary. If you are planning a surprise for someone, call it just that. A surprise. Sexual predators often say things like "This is our secret." Make your child understand they need to tell you if someone asks them to keep a secret. No matter what.

Another part of the plan is to get your kids to agree on some basic safety rules. If they're hanging around the neighborhood, they should always travel with a

7 ACTIONS YOU CAN TAKE TO KEEP YOUR **CHILD SAFE** FROM PREDATORS

1. Never, not even for a minute, leave your little one alone in a car. The same goes for a public place.
2. Don't put your child's name on their backpack, jackets or any other possessions. Children naturally let their guard down when they hear someone call their name.
3. Always accompany your little one to the public restroom.
4. It doesn't matter if she's trick-or-treating or selling Girl Scout cookies, never let your child go door-to-door in your neighborhood without you.
5. Always check all the windows and doors after a handyman, painter or other worker leaves your house and make sure they are closed and locked.
6. Ask about security at your child's school and don't be afraid to talk to administrators if you're not comfortable with their policies.
7. Get references for babysitters, tutors and anyone you hire to work in your home, like cleaning people, handymen or landscapers—and then call them. You may also want to do a background check.

friend or two. Insist they always use a sidewalk, which will make it more difficult for someone in a car to snatch them. If a sidewalk is not available, tell them to walk as far away from the curb as possible. It's also good practice to walk facing traffic so a car pulling up along side of them won't surprise them. If a car does pull up, advise your kids to run away toward the direction of the rear of the car. Putting a car in reverse quickly is harder to do than accelerating forward so the car will have difficulty following them.

What should your children do if someone grabs them? Tell them to grab something else. Grab whatever is in reach—a sign, a tree, another person—and don't let go. Or show them how to make large circles with their arms as if they are swimming. This makes it more difficult for someone to hold onto to them.

Finally, they should yell "Fire!" or "I'm being kidnapped!" because there's a good chance your neighbors are used to hearing playing children's screams and won't investigate unless they hear something unusual.

TEACH TRUST YOUR GUT

We all have a built-in alarm that's triggered when danger is lurking. It may take the form of a little voice telling you to beware or an icky feeling in the pit of your stomach. Our kids need to be reminded that if something doesn't seem right and even if they're not sure what it is, they should trust that feeling and get to safety.

They also need to be reminded that if this gut feeling, or instinct kicks in, all polite behavior rules are thrown out the window. This is one time when it's OK to say no to an adult and even be rude if something seems off.

MAKE A FAMILY PASSWORD

A family password is a secret phrase or code word known by you and your children only. It's a security measure your family uses if there's ever an emergency and you need to send someone to pick up your child but your child isn't expecting them. Once the person says the password, your child knows you have sent him and it's OK to go with him.

Having a family passwords also makes it difficult for a stranger to lure your child away. Not long ago, news reports told of a foiled kidnapping. A stranger approached two 8 year old boys in Utah after a scouting event. The man said he

was there because the boys' parents had asked him to pick them up. The boys asked for the password and the man didn't know it. It was instantly clear this was a dangerous situation and they ran back to the event to get help.

Choose a word or phrase that's simple to remember. Avoid words that are obvious to people outside of your family like the name of your dog or favorite sports team. Once you've chosen the word or phrase, use it only once. After it's used, choose a new password.

Technology

I'll admit I've entertained the thought of taking the iPad away. But I've since realized banning the Internet is not the answer. Kids will find a way to get access... usually through a friend. And technology is a huge part of school curriculums these days. So what can we do to ensure they have the safest experience possible? Teach them to be "technology smart". Set rules and guide them towards taking responsibility for their own safety online.

ESTABLISH RULES

Setting guidelines for technology use will help prevent your child from getting in trouble online. Start by keeping devices and gaming consoles where you can see them. Will you be able to casually walk by and see what's going on if the game consoles are on the basement TV? Same goes for the family computer. Pick a quiet—but not secluded spot—where your child can work. If your child has a mobile device or laptop, will you allow them to hide away in their room with it?

Decide on what is appropriate content and what isn't. For young children, you'll want to get familiar with the site first before you give them free rein to explore. Make a list of approved sites your kids can visit and games they can play. Be sure they understand any site or game that's not on the list requires special permission from you before they visit. Be prepared to adjust the restrictions as your child gets older. Is YouTube allowed? Do they need your permission before they register on a new website or download a new app? Set age appropriate rules and once the rules are established, be clear about the consequences. And always follow-through.

Decide on how much online time is appropriate. According to the Family Online Safety Institute, parents underestimate how much screen time their children get. While we think our children average two hours a day online, the real number is more like five. Set a time limit and stick to it.

Insist on Tech-Free Zones. Establish rules about when technology is not allowed. Can your child bring an electronic device to school? Will the phone or iPad be allowed at the dinner table? Is there a cut-off time when texting and face-timing isn't allowed? Will your child be required to surrender their device to you at bedtime so they don't stay up surfing the net all night?

TECHNOLOGY CONTRACTS

A technology contract spells out your rules and expectations. It holds your child accountable. If it's written down no one can say "I didn't know". Ultimately, a contract is more about starting a family conversation about technology than it is about getting it written on paper, however a documented agreement will keep everyone on the same page. Sit down with your child and go over the guidelines. In addition to approved websites, time limits and technology-free zones, you may want address the following:

- What kind of adult supervision or parental controls will you require, if any?
- What kind of personal information and photos can be shared on social media?
- Is downloading apps or making purchases online without permission allowed?
- What are your expectations for your child regarding the treatment of others while social media?
- Who is your child allowed to call and text?
- Who pays the phone bill?
- Is there a limit to how many texts can be sent in a day, week or month?
- What happens if a rule is broken?

During the discussion, you'll probably discover you will have a different set of rules for each device—cell phone, computer, gaming console. If that's the case, no problem. Draw up a technology contract for each one.

DISCUSS THE RISKS

Talk to your children regularly about online dangers like inappropriate content, online predators, loss of privacy and damaged reputations. Make sure they understand how these dangers could harm them.

→ INAPPROPRIATE CONTENT

There's a lot of stuff on the Internet that's inappropriate for kids and unfortunately, it's not too difficult for them to find it. Porn, violence and other sketchy material are only a click away. If you are worried about your children stumbling across content that could scar their innocent eyes, or your child has trouble adhering to your online time limit rule, consider using filters and monitoring tools. Parental controls are available for most devices. Check with your wireless and Internet service providers as well as your browser to see what's available and if it will meet your needs. If it's not enough, consider purchasing software like Net Nanny.

If you choose to use parental controls, just know they aren't perfect. There's still a chance an inappropriate website could get through. And they may do nothing to prevent information from going out so you'll still need to pay attention to how your child is using the Web.

→ ONLINE PREDATORS

According to research, the chance that your child will be harmed by someone they met online is slim. But my motto is it's better to be safe than sorry when it comes to my kids. I mean, why wouldn't you teach your kids basic Internet safety practices to ensure that a slim chance is slimmer?

Young kids should never give out personal information online whether it's their info, their brother or sister's or even yours. Make this a no-exceptions rule: Do not share your full name, age, phone number, email address, password, school, address or photo without permission from Mom or Dad.

As your child gets older, you may want to adjust this rule slightly. Who can your child give information to and what information is allowed? For example, you may decide it's OK for your teen to give out their email address, but home address is still not allowed.

Caution your tweens and teens against talking about sex with anyone online and be sure they understand they should never get together with someone they met over the Internet without your permission. Then tell them why so they will understand the possible consequences of their actions.

What do you do if you've discussed online predators with your child but you have a feeling something is going on? Don't ignore it. Talk to your child and don't hesitate to ask plenty of questions.

→ LOSS OF PRIVACY

Children are impulsive and spontaneous and that can work against them to when it comes to preserving their privacy online. It's not unusual for kids to share information or photos that are embarrassing to themselves or the family without thinking *Is this TMI*? In addition, they freely give out all sorts of private information—name, birth date, or your credit card number—every time they open a social media account, download an app, or shop online.

Start a conversation about keeping private information private and the risks like online identity theft, behavioral marketing, and fraud. Instruct your child to avoid contests, giveaways and questionnaires as these are created to collect personal information. Be sure to turn off the GPS settings on all devices that give away your child's location. Some mobile apps collect personal information, including location, calendar and contacts. To find out what information is collected and how it's shared, scan the app permissions and decide if it's right for your child before he downloads it. If your son or daughter is active on social networks, set the privacy settings on the accounts yourself and occasionally check to make sure your child hasn't changed them.

Educate your child about the consequences of clicking links in emails from unknown senders, opening up web pages that contain viruses, and phishing

scams that try to trick people into giving personal information or money.

Also teach your child how to create a strong password. No pets' names or birthdates, please! For the best protection, use a different password on each account. Make sure your child understands that passwords are not to be shared with anyone—not boyfriends, girlfriends and even best friends—for any reason, period.

→ REPUTATION

Think back to your teen years and you'll probably be grateful Facebook didn't exist. We all have at least one thing in our past we'd just as soon erase from our memory. Now, imagine if that memory is forever archived online and someone can pull it up and share it on social media!

If your thinking privacy settings will protect your son or daughter, think again. Nothing on the Internet is ever really private. The reality is they've lost control the moment they clicked share. Even if you go back and delete the comment or photo, you don't know who has already copied, pasted, and saved it with the intention of sharing at a later date.

Kids have been kicked off sports teams because they've posted inappropriate photos or comments to social media. Even worse, some have been in trouble with the law for sexting. Talk to your teen and help him understand that everything he says online and anything anyone else says about him leaves a digital footprint that can't be erased. Encourage him to think twice before he tweets or texts. A good way he can measure if it's appropriate is to ask himself, would I do or say this in person in front of my parents, grandparents, college admissions officer, or employer? If the answer is no then he shouldn't do it online. Remind him there are no "take-backs." Once it's posted, it's forever out there.

BE INVOLVED

With little ones, being involved will most likely mean sitting next to them while they are online. There's no doubt, it can be painful to spend an hour clicking around PBS Kids but it's the best way teach online safety to young kids while making sure they stay safe.

Older children will balk at the idea of you looking over their shoulder but you still should be involved in their online world. Chances are they know more about what's out there in the techno world than you do, but try to be informed about websites, social media and apps your child uses. I can't count the number of phone calls I've received from a friend giving me a heads up to the latest and greatest social networks in our tweens' digital world. I mean why does Snapchat have to arrive on the scene when I'm just getting the hang of Instagram? Asking your child to teach you is the easiest way to learn. Be genuinely interested as they show you what they do online and ask questions.

One of the best ways to stay on top of your child's online activity is to get on social media yourself and friend or follow them. Be prepared for your son or daughter to not like this idea but don't give in. Having access to your child's page helps you stay on top of what's posted and it should cause your child to think twice before he posts something questionable. But do your child a favor. Once you've been let into his corner of the web, stay invisible. Commenting on posts or sharing photos will only embarrass him.

In my house, we have a no-password rule. I want to be pick up my daughter's iPad and have access to her social media at any time. Even with no password on the device, there are still plenty of websites with passwords. I recommend you get a list of the log-ons and passwords for all social media accounts and websites your child uses and explain you will only use the access in an emergency.

Lastly, being involved means being approachable. When your child comes to you with an Internet problem whether it's inappropriate content or a nasty message from a so-called friend, stay calm and help them navigate through it. If you want to keep the lines of communication open, the worst thing you can do is punish them by banning the Internet.

BE A GOOD ROLE MODEL

Now it's time to turn the mirror onto yourself. Are you constantly on your cell phone or iPad? Follow your own rules and turn off the technology. You can't expect your child to strike a balance with his usage when you're not able to yourself. Remember, you are a role model so if you're doing something—like texting and driving—you can expect your kids to follow suit.

Guns

How to teach kids about guns is almost as controversial as the guns themselves. Some parents believe the way to teach children to be safe around guns is to expose them to guns. If you teach young kids to shoot and how to properly handle a gun, their curiosity diminishes. Then if they find one, they will be less likely to play with it.

Other parents educate their kids about the dangers of guns and teach them to never touch a gun. Some schools are taking this stance and are implementing gun safety programs in their curriculum, like The Eddie Eagle GunSafe Program. Developed by a task force of teachers, law enforcement personnel, and psychologists, this program is available to parents through the National Rifle Association. The program includes tools to teach kids one message: If you find a gun, stop! Don't touch. Leave the area. Tell an adult.

HOW TO **ASK OTHER PARENTS** IF THERE IS A GUN IN THEIR HOUSE

You've taken safety precautions to keep your kids safe from guns in your home and you assume your child's friend's parents have to, but are you certain? The only way you can find out for sure is to ask before you send your little one over to play. Here are some tips to make asking less awkward:

- **Ask the other parent when the kids aren't around.** Some parents aren't comfortable talking about guns in front of their children.
- **Don't make it about gun ownership.** Make it about gun safety. Instead of "Do you have a gun in your house?", ask "If you have a gun, do you keep it locked and stored away?"
- **Don't make a big deal about asking.** Think of it as just another question on the list of details you need to discuss before the playdate and work it into your casual conversation.
- **Don't worry about offending the other parent.** Most parents will understand you're just looking out for your child's safety and should not be offended by the question.

Unfortunately, studies have shown that many children who have been trained not to touch a gun still can't resist. The only guaranteed way to prevent your kids from a gun accident is to keep your guns unloaded and locked away. Store unloaded firearms in a locked cabinet, gun vault or safe. Store the ammunition in a separate locked location. Hiding a gun in a drawer or on the top shelf of your closest is not safe. Kids are experts at finding things we think are hidden from them.

Even if the guns in your home are stored safely away from little hands, you can't assume every gun owner takes the same precautions. Therefore you still need to talk to your children about the dangers of guns. Talk about what they should do if they see a gun when away from home. Quiz them regularly. Make a lesson out of the violence you see on television and in video games. Stress how it differs from violence in real life.

Bullies

Bullying is when one kid tries to have power over another by repeatedly being mean or hurtful. Bullies may physically or verbally attack, threaten or spread rumors about their victims. Intentionally excluding someone from a group is also an example of bullying.

Kids who bully may have never learned it's not right to pick on others who are different. Or they may feel insecure and preying on weaker kids makes them feel better about themselves. Sometimes kids bully because they have difficulty managing their own feelings of anger, hurt, and frustration.

HOW TO PREVENT BULLYING

Starting when your kids are young, teach them to be kind and respectful of others. Make sure your kids understand that making fun of people who are different is wrong. Look for opportunities, like community service projects, to expose your children to a variety of people.

Talk to your kids about bullying. Explain what it is and let them know they can come to you for help if they feel bullied. Also encourage them to intervene if they see other kids being picked on.

Encourage your kids to get involved in group activities and hobbies outside of school. They will build relationships with others who have similar interests and at the same time build their confidence.

Be there for your children. Kids are more likely to come to you with a problem if they feel like the door is always open. Plan an activity to do together on a regular basis or set aside ten or 15 minutes each day just to talk. Find out what their life is like. Ask questions like "Who did you sit with at lunch?" or "What good things happened today?"

WHAT DO I DO IF MY CHILD IS BULLIED?

Hopefully, your child will come to you if he is bullied at school but sometimes kids feel ashamed of what's happening or worry you'll be disappointed so they keep it to themselves. Here are signs your child may be dealing with bullies and isn't telling you:

- Has bruises, cuts, scrapes or other injuries that can't be explained
- Regularly loses or breaks toys, clothes, books, electronics or jewelry with no explanation
- Complains of frequent headaches or stomachaches and takes regular trips to the school nurse
- Eats more or eats less
- Changes in sleep habits or experiencing nightmares
- Drop in grade performance
- Doesn't want to go to school
- Refuses to ride the school bus
- Disinterested in friends and avoids social activities
- Change in mood, decreased self esteem, feeling helpless
- Harms themselves, runs away or is suicidal

If your child is the target of bullies, there are some things you can do to help. First, stay calm. Listen to your child tell you what's happening and how they feel about it. Don't freak out or your child may not feel comfortable coming to you in the future. Gather as much information as you can about what's happening, when it's happening, and how long it's been happening.

Help your child come up with strategies to deal with the bullying on his own. Start a conversation about ways he can handle it, like walking away or acting unaffected. Bullies thrive on reactions. It makes them feel powerful. If they aren't getting a rise out of your child they may stop. Don't advise him to "hit back" as this could make the situation worse or result in your child getting suspended or expelled. Identify people at school that he can go to for help. Once your child has decided on a strategy, practice it. Role play will increase your child's confidence.

If the bullying continues, contact the school. Arrange a meeting with the teacher and principal and calmly, inform them of the facts. Let them know you're willing to work with them to resolve the situation. Learn about the school's anti-bullying policies and find out what they plan to do. Set a follow-up appointment to check on their progress.

WHAT DO I DO IF MY CHILD IS THE BULLY?

None of us wants to admit our child could be a bully but it's important we recognize the signs so we can do something about it.

- Gets into trouble at school
- Acts out aggressively
- Hangs out with other bullies
- Worries about reputation or popularity
- Is overly competitive
- Blames others instead of taking responsibility for own actions
- Has extra money and new stuff but can't explain where it came from

If you've gotten the dreaded call from school that your child has been involved in a bullying incident, there are a few steps you need to take. First, establish a no-bullying rule for home and school. Let your child know that you will not tolerate the behavior and there will be serious consequences. Then be sure you follow through immediately if you learn he is involved in an incident.

Talk to your child and try to find out why he's doing it. If he tries to pass the blame onto someone else, tell him you want to hear about his role in the incident only. Then encourage empathy by asking him how he would feel in the victim's shoes. Together, come up with a way he can apologize to the victim.

Find out what others think about your child's behavior. Teachers, guidance counselors and administrators may be able to shed some light on what's happening at school. Is your child struggling with anger? Who is your child hanging around with? Look for anything that could be influencing the behavior.

Then look at your own behavior. How do you talk to your kids? Do you have trouble managing your anger? Are you able to work through conflicts with others? Your kids are learning how to treat others by watching you. If yelling, name calling, putdowns and harsh criticism are a norm in your house, your kids may think these learned behaviors are acceptable anywhere.

Most importantly, if the bullying doesn't stop, reach out to a counselor for help.

Cyberbullying

Cyberbullying is using technology to bully someone. One child harasses, threatens or embarrasses another through emails, text messages, interactive games, or on social media. Cyberbullying can be more upsetting than in-person bullying for several reasons. First, victims feel like they can't escape the bullies because cyberbullying can happen anywhere at anytime. Also, the aggression may be more extreme because kids will often say things online they would never say face-to-face. And many times the harassment is anonymous so it's difficult to trace.

If your child is the target of cyberbullies there are some things you can do. First, as tempting as it is, don't take away your child's technology. Many victims will hide cyberbullying from their parents for fear of losing online access. Print or save all emails, texts or posts for evidence. Block the bully from contacting your child via the cell phone provider. Do the same thing on social media channels. Then, take the same steps for handling in-person bullying. Don't respond to harassment, involve the bully's parents and school. You may have to take it one step further and report it the police as cyberbullies can sometimes be guilty of cyberstalking and other technology-related crimes.

Resources

The websites, suppliers, and blogs listed here represent by no means all of the resources to help you become survival savvy; they are simply the ones I often refer to and recommend. To find more resources, spend some time browsing the internet. Google terms like survival, preparedness, or disaster readiness.

WEBSITES:

- Ready: **ready.gov**
- Federal Emergency Management Agency: **fema.gov**
- Department of Homeland Security: **dhs.gov**
- Centers for Disease Control and Prevention: **cdc.gov**
- Department of Health & Human Services: **hhs.gov**
- National Weather Service (NOAA): **weather.gov**
- American Red Cross: **redcross.org**
- National Fire Protection Association: **nfpa.org**

SURVIVAL GEAR SUPPLIERS:

Emergency Essentials
800-999-1863
beprepared.com

The Ready Store
800-773-5331
thereadystore.com

Nitro-Pak Preparedness Center
800-866-4876
nitro-pak.com

Amazon
amazon.com

FOOD STORAGE SUPPLIERS:

Mountain House
800-547-0244
mountainhouse.com

Legacy Food Storage
888-543-7345
buyemergencyfoods.com

Augason Farms
800-878-0099
augasonfarms.com

Honeyville Grain
888-810-3212
honeyville.com

Thrive Life
877-743-5373
thrivelife.com

SURVIVAL AND PREPAREDNESS BLOGS:

- Are We Crazy or What?: **arewecrazyorwhat.net**
- Backdoor Survival: **backdoorsurvival.com**
- Common Sense Homesteading: **commonsensehome.com**
- Home Ready Home: **homereadyhome.com**
- Food Storage and Survival: **foodstorageandsurvival.com**
- Food Storage Made Easy: **foodstoragemadeeasy.net**
- Food Storage Moms: **foodstoragemoms.com**
- Graywolf Survival: **graywolfsurvival.com**
- Mom With a Prep: **momwithaprep.com**
- Peak Prosperity: **peakprosperity.com**
- Prepared Housewives: **prepared-housewives.com**
- Preparedness Mama: **preparednessmama.com**
- PrepperWebsite: **prepperwebsite.com**
- Survival Sherpa: **survivalsherpa.wordpress.com**
- The Busy B Homemaker: **thebusybhomemaker.com**
- The Survival Mom: **thesurvivalmom.com**
- Willow Haven Outdoor: **willowhavenoutdoor.com**

ABOUT THE AUTHOR

Julie Sczerbinski, is a Coach-purse carrying, Go-Bag packing wife and mom of two living in the suburbs of Charlotte, North Carolina. When she's not shopping at Super Target, she spends her time imagining possible emergency scenarios and plotting ways to tackle them. She is the creator of Home Ready Home (www.homereadyhome.com), a popular blog geared toward helping modern families become survival-savvy and build a more self-reliant life. Julie has been featured in *The Charlotte Observer* and interviewed on several preparedness podcasts. Her work as a writer has been published in local, regional and national publications such as *Breathe, Animal Wellness and Natural Health.*